BASEBALL

Wit and Wisdom

Folklore of a National Pastime

BOOKS BY FRANK GRAHAM

LOU GEHRIG, A QUIET HERO
THE NEW YORK YANKEES
McGRAW OF THE GIANTS
THE BROOKLYN DODGERS
AL SMITH, AMERICAN
THE NEW YORK GIANTS
THIRD MAN IN THE RING

BOOKS BY DICK HYMAN

IT'S THE LAW
IT'S AGAINST THE LAW
MARINE COMEDY
OF ALL FOOL THINGS
NONSENSE USA
IT'S STILL THE LAW

BASEBALL
Wit and Wisdom

Folklore of a National Pastime

By FRANK GRAHAM
and
DICK HYMAN

DAVID McKAY COMPANY, INC.

New York

BASEBALL WIT AND WISDOM

The authors gratefully acknowledge permission to use the following copyrighted material: Cartoon page 5 © 1962 O. Soglow; Cartoons pages 11, 31, 113, 135, 149, 165, 175, 191, 201, 207, 221, 259, © 1962 Bill Gallo, New York Daily News; Cartoon on page 25 © 1962 King Features Syndicate, Inc.; Cartoons pages 41, 45, 63, 75, © 1962 Murray Olderman, Newspaper Enterprise Ass'n., Inc.; Cartoon page 103 © 1962 Bob Dunn, King Features Syndicate Inc.; Cartoon page 110 © 1962 Burris Jenkins Jr., Hearst Headline Service; Cartoon page 126 © 1962 Schulz, United Feature Syndicate; Cartoon page 155 © 1962 Willard Mullin, N. Y. World-Telegram & Sun; Cartoon page 251 © 1962 Jimmy Hatlo, King Features Syndicate, Inc.; LIFE WITH FATHER by Bill Slocum © 1962 New York Chapter, Baseball Writers' Association of America; CONFESSIONS OF A BASEBALL FAN by John Hutchens, reprinted from the New York Times Magazine, July 14, 1946 by permission of the New York Times and the author; SOUTH AMERICA TAKE IT AWAY by Buck Canel © 1962 New York Chapter Baseball Writers' Association of America; FUN CAN BE BASEBALL © 1962 by Bugs Baer; excerpt from THE UMPIRE STORY © 1953 by James M. Kahn; excerpt from article by Clarence Woodbury in American Magazine May 1941 © Crowell Collier Publishing Co.; excerpt from BALL PLAYERS HAVE THEIR SUPERSTITIONS by H. L. Masin © 1942 Scholastic Magazines, Inc.; excerpt from BALL PLAYERS AND BUGABOOS by Raymond Schuessler © 1956 American Mercury; I REMEMBER © 1962 by Senator Ford

The grateful editors/authors of this book wish to dedicate the volume to many, many friends without whose help this—of all books—could never have been published.

Contents

Acknowledgments

LEE ALLEN, Historian of Baseball Hall of Fame, Cooperstown, N. Y.
ARTHUR "BUGS" BAER, Columnist, *Kings Features Syndicate*
JOHN BARRINGTON, former Sports Editor, *International News Service*
GEORGE A. BARTON, Sports Editor Emeritus, *Minneapolis Tribune*
BELIEVE IT OR NOT, INC.
JACK BERGER, Pittsburgh Pirates
DON BIEBEL, Chicago Cubs
LES BIEDERMAN, *Pittsburgh Press*
CLEM BODDINGTON
BUCK CANEL
LAWTON CARVER, *New York Herald Tribune*
BOB CHANDLER, Philadelphia Phillies
HAROLD "SPIKE" CLAASSEN, *Associated Press*
TIM COHANE, Sports Editor, *Look Magazine*
BOB CONSIDINE, *Hearst Headline Service*
BILL CROWLEY, Boston Red Sox
DONALD DAVIDSON, Milwaukee Braves
ARTHUR DALEY, Sports Columnist, *The New York Times*
JIMMY DOYLE, *Cleveland Plain Dealer*
BOB DUNN, Cartoonist, creator of "Just My Type"
JACK DUNN, Baltimore Orioles
JIMMY DURANTE
MEL DURSLAG, *Los Angeles Examiner*
CHARLES EINSTEIN, *San Francisco Examiner*
JOE FALLS, *Detroit Free Press*
BARRY FARIS, Former Editor, *International News Service*

JAMES A. FARLEY
LEO FISCHER, *Chicago American*
BOB FISCHEL, New York Yankees
SENATOR ED FORD, Humorist
OSCAR FRALEY, Sports Columnist, *United Press International*
PAUL FREHM, artist for Ripley's "Believe It or Not" feature
HUGH FULLERTON, Sports Columnist, *Associated Press*
BILL GALLO, Cartoonist, *New York Daily News*
BILL GILBERT, Washington Senators
RAY GRODY, Milwaukee Braves
JIMMY HATLO, Cartoonist, creator of "They'll Do It Every Time"
HERB HEFT, Minnesota Twins
HARRY HERSHFIELD, Humorist and Columnist
HY HURWITZ, *Boston Globe*
BURRIS JENKINS, Cartoonist, *New York Journal American*
JAMES M. KAHN, author of "The Umpire Story"
MAX KASE, Sports Editor, *New York Journal American*
IRV KAZE, Los Angeles Angels
King Features Syndicate
BOB MAISEL, *Baltimore Sun*
H. L. MASIN
JIM McCULLY, *New York Daily News*
JACK McDONALD, *San Francisco News Call Bulletin*
TOM MEANY, New York Mets
HAL MIDDLESWORTH, Detroit Tigers
WILLARD MULLIN, Cartoonist, *New York World Telegram & Sun*
MURRAY OLDERMAN, Cartoonist, *Newspaper Enterprise Association*
JOSEPH M. OVERFIELD
DAN PARKER, Sports Editor, *New York Daily Mirror*
ARTHUR PATTERSON, Los Angeles Dodgers
LEO PATERSON, Sports Editor, *United Press International*
SHIRLEY POVICH, *Washington, D.C., Post Times Herald*
HOWARD ROBERTS, Chicago White Sox
FRED RUSSELL, *Nashville Banner*
AL SCHACHT, "Clown Prince" of baseball
RAYMOND SCHUESSLER
JIM SCHAAF, Kansas City Athletics
GARRY SCHUMACHER, San Francisco Giants

CHARLES M. SCHULZ, Cartoonist, creator of "Peanuts"
TOM SEEBERG, Los Angeles Dodgers
TOOTS SHOR
FRANK SLOCUM
BILL SLOCUM, Columnist, *New York Daily Mirror*
CHET SMITH, *Pittsburgh Press*
OTTO SOGLOW, Cartoonist, creator of "The Little King"
C. C. JOHNSON SPINK, *The Sporting News*
FRANCIS STANN, *Washington, D. C., Star*
JIM TOOMEY, St. Louis Cardinals
NATE WALLACK, Cleveland Indians
GENE WARD, Sports Columnist, *New York Daily News*
CLARENCE WOODBURY, *New York Daily News*
HANK ZUREICK, Cincinnati Reds

Foreword

BY FRANK GRAHAM

"Tell me," the young man said, "about baseball."

"What is it you wish to know?" the old man countered.

"About how and where it began, for instance," the young man said.

"You will have to ask someone older than I," the old man said. "See if you can find a man a couple of thousand years old and ask him."

"Surely," the young man said, "you are joshing."

"Only to a degree," the old man said. "What I mean is that while I have been around for a long while and have read a great deal about baseball, in which I always have been interested, I have not come upon the writings of any historians who know all the answers. Fortunately, they have been frank enough to admit this. Briefly, their research leads them back to their starting point . . . by the way, are you listening?"

"Oh, yes!" the young man said.

"I thought," the old man said, "I detected you nodding and, if you are, you have good reason to do so but I must say, in self-defense, that you asked for it. . . . Well, trying to determine who invented baseball, and where, is akin to asking who invented the ball. Who invented the stick with

xiii

which to hit the ball? Who invented running? These learned scholars believe that stick-and-ball games from which, ultimately, the game we call 'baseball' was derived, originated with the Egyptians in a kind of . . . I gather . . . bruising religious ceremony, in which the object was to hit either a ball or other worshipers' skulls with a bludgeon. If I sound somewhat unclear on that point, so do the scholars.

"Anyhow, a game slightly resembling baseball was known in France, where it was called 'poison ball,' though why it was so called I have not been able to discover. Then, in England there was a game called 'rounders.' This was brought to America and immediately gained favor, especially in New England, where it was known as either 'rounders' or 'town ball.' And from that beginning it grew into what we call 'baseball,' and after a while we developed men named Harry Wright and George Wright, brothers . . . although not to be confused with the Wright brothers who got a flying machine off the ground at Kitty Hawk . . . and John McGraw and Willie Keeler and Tinkers-to-Evers-to-Chance and Ty Cobb and Babe Ruth and Joe DiMaggio and Stan Musial and Mickey Mantle and Casey Stengel and Whitey Ford and Yogi Berra."

"But," the young man asked, "wasn't there a man named Abner Doubleday? I thought he invented baseball."

"Yes," the old man said. "There also was a character called Santa Claus, who is supposed to have invented the giving of gifts at Christmastide."

"But," the young man said, "the way I heard it, Abner Doubleday invented baseball at Cooperstown, New York, and that is why the National Hall of Fame and Museum is at Cooperstown and is the shrine of baseball. How about that?"

" 'How about that' is a good question," the old man said.

"I will try to answer it. The mystery of the origin of baseball was as deep in 1905 as it is now and Albert G. Spalding, who had been a great baseball player in his youth and subsequently became even more famous as a manufacturer of baseball equipment and the publisher of *Spalding's Baseball Guide,* took it upon himself to appoint a committee, headed by General A. G. Mills, briefly president of the National League in the eighties, to make a thorough study of the problem. The committee fumbled—pardon, I should have said it deliberated—for two years and came up with a pronouncement that baseball was invented by Abner Doubleday, a Cooperstown schoolboy, in 1839. This was accepted by Spalding, who was powerful enough to override any objection to his decision, although one of the dissenters was English-born Henry Chadwick, the first baseball writer and now, ironically, enshrined at Cooperstown—ironically, I say, because he loudly protested that the decision of the Mills Committee was pure balderdash, since, as a boy in England, he had played rounders, and this thing they called baseball was but a glorified version of the game he'd known as a toddler."

"But," said the young man, "why did Spalding . . . ?"

"That," the old man said, "I don't know. Maybe he just wanted it that way. Robert W. Henderson, a true baseball student and historian, reviewing at a later date the evidence weighed by the Mills Committee, discovered that the basis of its report was a letter written by one Abner Graves, then in his eighties, to the effect that, in 1839, he had seen a fellow schoolboy in Cooperstown, named Abner Doubleday, draw an outline of a diamond on a field and instruct other schoolboys how the game should be played. There were some discrepancies in his story. In 1839, for instance, Doubleday was not a schoolboy in Cooperstown. He was a West Point

cadet. He rose to the rank of general in the Union Army and
served with distinction during the Civil War. After he retired
he devoted his life to writing for newspapers and magazines,
but not once, according to Henderson, did he mention baseball. When he died in November of 1893, no mention was
made in his *New York Times* obituary of any connection he
may have had with baseball. Mr. Henderson surmises that,
had General Doubleday lived until 1907 and read the report
of the Mills Committee, he would have been astonished."

"Wasn't there," the young man persisted, "somebody
named Cartwright who had something to do with the invention—pardon me, the development—of baseball?"

"Now," the old man said, "you are on firmer ground. Yes,
there was. His name was Alexander Joy Cartwright, Jr., and
he, too, has his niche at Cooperstown. It says on his plaque:

" 'Father of Modern Baseball. Set the bases 90 feet apart.
Established 9 innings as a game and 9 players as a team.
Organized the Knickerbocker Baseball Club of New York in
1845. Carried baseball to Pacific Coast and Hawaii in pio-
neer days.' "

"How do you know all this?" the young man asked.

"I just read it in a book by John Durant, called *The Story
of Baseball,* published by Hastings House in 1947. John is a
very good friend of mine and he is the one who tipped me
off to Mr. Henderson."

"Then Cooperstown is a fraud?" the young man asked.

"No," the old man said. "It is a legend, and one of the
finest legends in all this broad land of ours. It is a lovely
town which, in all its loveliness, is being carefully preserved
. . . its old streets, its old homes, the beauty of the shore
lines of Otsego Lake, which James Fenimore Cooper called
'Glimmer Glass.' It is a town that will not have to be restored
as, for instance, Williamsburg, Virginia, was. It is now as it

was and always will be, and if General Mills had to fake a setting for the origin of baseball, let us say for him that there was a touch of genius in his choice."

"Anything more to say?" the young man asked.

"Yes," the old man said. "Get to bed."

Introduction

BY RED SMITH

Ping Bodie, an outfielder of high repute and deliberate speed, was thrown out trying to steal second base. "His heart was full of larceny," wrote Bugs Baer, "but his feet were honest."

"Then Koenig got a hit," Ring Lardner reported from the 1927 World Series, "on a ground ball that would of been an easy out for any first baseman that was not quite so much of a recluse as Joe Harris."

In 1913 Frank Chance, manager of the Yankees, traded the dexterous and devious Hal Chase to the White Sox for Rollie Zeider, a third baseman with a bunion so tender he could scarcely walk, and Babe Borton, a first baseman with two sound left feet. "Chance," wrote Mark Roth in the *New York Globe,* "traded Chase for a bunion and an onion."

Bob Meusel, a dour outfielder with the Yankees, showed signs of mellowing as age dimmed his talents. "He's learning to say hello," Frank Graham wrote, "when it's time to say good-by."

All of which sets a fellow to wondering: What is the source of baseball's imperishable popularity in America? Is it the drama inherent in the competition? Is it the poetry of motion on what Thomas Wolfe called "the velvet geometry" of the diamond? Or is it the literature of the game, past and present?

Sometimes I think that the Charley Drydens and Heywood Brouns, the Tommy Holmeses and Dick Youngs, have contributed more to the sport with their typewriters than Babe Ruth and Ty Cobb did with their bats. Or at least as much.

One thing I know for sure: Nobody who ever despoiled a virgin sheet of copy paper has contributed more to the profession of sports reporting or to the pleasure of sports reading than Frank Graham.

Singlehanded, and with no thought of doing anything of the kind, he revolutionized the approach to writing a sports column. When he inherited the late Joe Vila's space in the *New York Sun,* most sports page columns were personal essays of editorial comment, forums for debate on topics in the news. Appointment as columnist did not, in Frank's opinion, invest him with infallibility or even judicial authority.

"I am a reporter," he told himself, though probably not in so many words. "My job is to take the reader by the arm, usher him into places he cannot visit in person—the baseball dugout, the jockeys' quarters at the track, the fighter's dressing room—where he can hear what is said and see what is done behind the scenes."

Frank would never claim invention of the "conversation piece" type of column. But if he wasn't the first to use it, he did elevate it to a quality never approached until he came quietly around with his tact and taste and understanding, his fantastically accurate ear for dialogue and his marvelous ability to evoke an image.

He never tried to tell anybody how to write a sports column, but he showed everybody how. As he is still showing them today in the *New York Journal-American* and here in collaboration with Dick Hyman.

RED SMITH

WIRE MILL ROAD
STAMFORD, CONN.

XX

I. Jinxes and Jonahs

The Superstitions of Ballplayers On and Off the Field

BY DICK HYMAN

"He that is without superstition among you, let him cast the first stone."

The true origin of superstition is to be found in early man's effort to explain nature and his own existence; in the desire to propitiate Fate and invite Fortune; in the wish to avoid evils he could not understand; and in the unavoidable attempt to pry into the future.

Like sin and the common cold, superstition has few open advocates. Nevertheless, we have a big red-plush-covered hunch that a universal Gallup poll would indicate that a trifle more than 99 per cent of the human race have an unknown quantity of superstition germs perpetually perambulating among their red and white corpuscles.

Baseball players as a whole are superstitious about their superstitions. They admit they have them, but they dislike to talk about them.

1

Here are a few of the baseball superstitions that are accepted generally by players:

A ballplayer in a hitting streak will wear the same sweat shirt until it is mildewed.

A player always tips his hat to a truckload of empty barrels, but they must be empty; and always tips his hat to a load of hay.

A no-hitter is never discussed while it is in process. And, on such an occasion, the players go far afield to find other topics of conversation.

When a team gets into a batting slump, someone will toss the bats around for a change of luck.

Joe Dugan, one of the greatest third basemen of all time, would never throw a ball to a pitcher unless it was for an actual putout. When Joe was with the Yankees, it was a great trick for the players to throw the ball around the infield and when Dugan got the ball they all would turn their backs to him, while the pitcher stood with outstretched hands waiting for the ball. Dugan's answer to this was to walk across the infield and hand the ball to the pitcher. But throw it—*never*.

Babe Ruth always touched second base on his way in from the outfield.

Phil Rizzuto made the same design on the plate every time he came up to bat.

When going out to play the outfield from the bench, Joe DiMaggio always stubbed his toe in some particular place.

Eddie Collins always carried a wad of chewing gum on the button of his cap, and when two strikes were called on him, he would take down the gum and chew it vigorously for good luck.

Lefty O'Doul wore green suits for good luck.

Big league players are more superstitious than your Aunt Kate. To them, hex isn't an unknown quantity in algebra, but something real and tangible that they feel can put the creeping death on their batting average or pixillate their won and lost record if they don't humor it. Sometimes they can pamper one of these pet superstitions until it grows into a real Frankenstein; thus Al Lopez, the catcher, ate kippered herring and eggs for breakfast 17 days in a row, because he happened to be on a hitting streak. To change the diet, Al felt, would be to change his luck, and hence change those base hits into outs.

Leo Durocher erases the chalk lines in the coaching box with his spikes. He is also superstitious about clothes. He would wear the same shirt, the same suit, if his team was on a winning streak.

There is a lot of voodoo connected with gloves. Many pitchers, as they come off the mound, are careful to leave their mitts on the turf with the fingers pointing in a certain direction. Lefty Gomez would never let anybody hand him his glove as he took the field.

Opposing players got wise to this and would be over-polite, picking up Lefty's glove from its resting place near the foul line. But he would never accept it. If anybody offered his glove, Lefty kept his hands behind his back until the player dropped it.

Hughey Critz always made a ritual of touching his rival second baseman's glove as it lay in the field before he picked up his own at the start of an inning. Critz was most superstitious. His pockets were always filled with the oddest collection of twine, wire and broken glass. He would search for these things on the field, as if they were gold. He was allergic to small pieces of torn paper.

George Stallings, manager, was infuriated by small pieces of paper and peanut shells. He felt that they jinxed his team. Stallings went a bit further than worriers who stuck to the same clothes or diet; he would keep the position he happened to be in when his team made a base hit; he wanted to encourage a rally this way. Once Stallings happened to be in a stooping position, retrieving a peanut shell, when one of the 1914 Braves made a hit. He stayed in that cramped position while ten men went to bat, in what proved to be a rousing rally. Stallings got his runs but he also got his miseries from his lumbago. The trainer had to untangle his muscles after two of the Miracle Man's players helped him to the clubhouse.

Casey Stengel believes that picking up a stray hairpin denotes a two-base hit. Dixie Walker picked up three hairpins one day and followed his luck with three base hits that afternoon. John McGraw had a standing rule in his family that baseball never was mentioned at the dinner table on any day the Giants lost.

Seeing a cross-eyed girl on the way to the park meant no hits. Some players have shied from a table when they saw even a partly cross-eyed waitress approach to take their orders.

4

SOME PLAYERS HAVE SHIED FROM A TABLE
WHEN THEY SAW EVEN A PARTLY CROSS-EYED
WAITRESS APPROACH TO TAKE THEIR ORDER.

5

At the first sign of a players' fight, **George** Selkirk always ran in to first base, lifted the bag and put his expensive dental plate under it for safekeeping. Then waded in.

All ballplayers have a horror of having a man's hat placed on a bed.

During the spring **Ty** Cobb used to practice with lead-weighted shoes, then put on his paper-thin ones the first day of the season. He believed that this made him faster on the base paths.

Jake Powell, once of the Yankees and Senators, believed that every time he found a hairpin he'd get a hit. He found 208 in one season, his last in the minors, and got 208 hits that year. One day while in a slump, he followed a stout Negro lady for three miles, waiting for one of those big bone hairpins to fall out of her hair. It finally fell. Jake grabbed it, raced to the ball park, and broke his slump with a triple the first time up.

Waitresses complain that ballplayers believe it is unlucky to leave more than a quarter tip.

Many baseball pitchers will refuse to step on a crack in a sidewalk on the day they are to pitch. If it is a sidewalk with many cracks, they walk in the road all the way to the ball park. If a black cat crosses their path, players will turn around and drive or walk blocks to avoid the cat. Players dislike starting a trip on a Friday, figuring it will be disastrous, and so the schedule makers avoid this as much as possible. They are also superstitious about breaking mirrors, walking under ladders, and carrying pictures of their mothers-in-law.

7

Babe Ruth had a superstition that he must wash out his eyes before each game. He had a special bottle of eyewash for this purpose. One day in Detroit he forgot to wash his eyes until just before the game, and he sent a bat boy for the bottle. The trainer had switched bottles in some manner and Babe washed his eyes thoroughly with turpentine. Yelling like a bull, Babe applied cold water to the stinging eyes. Oh, yes, he got a home run and two doubles that day!

Eddie Mathews, of the Milwaukee Braves, always makes sure of touching third base when he returns to his position from the dugout.

Gil Hodges has always thrown a kiss to his wife in the stands after hitting a home run.

Walter Alston never touches the base line when going to the mound to talk to a pitcher.

Pitcher Don Drysdale avoids the base line when walking on or off the mound.

Frank Howard, when entering the batter's box, makes an extended reach over the plate, touching the far corner with his bat, and then resumes his natural stance.

* * *

Here are some superstitions as revealed by Eddie Froelich, trainer of the Chicago White Sox; he also served with the Red Sox and the Yankees:

Vic Raschi, after a hitter had been retired, would stand poker-faced on the mound, looking at the third baseman and

8

not following the flight of the ball around the infield. The ball *had* to be returned by the third baseman while Raschi was standing on the mound.

Most ballplayers use the same bat while in a hitting streak. Joe Gordon was just the reverse. He'd change bats every trip to the plate.

The Yankees of the Joe DiMaggio days would always wait for DiMag to lead the charge onto the field for the game. It was their silent tribute to the King.

Dick Donovan, on the day he pitches, always sits in a certain place on the bench, spits tobacco juice at one certain spot, folds his towel just so, talks to no one, and wants no one sitting close to him.

Many veteran players cling steadfastly to an old glove which served them in their glory days. Some gloves are actually rotted with age and perspiration.

* * *

Clarence Woodbury reported on certain events in an article in the *American Magazine* back in May, 1941:

As Lusty Lou Novikoff, the so-called mad Russian of baseball, stepped to the plate one afternoon, a feminine voice rose piercingly from the front row of the grandstand.

"Strike the big bum out!" the woman screamed. "Strike him out!"

A startled fan nudged the man next to him. "Who's the dame?" he asked.

"She's sure got it in for him, whoever she is."

"She has like heck!" replied the other fan. "That's Lou's wife. He always has her sit up front and call him a bum when he goes to bat. He's kind of superstitious that way."

Novikoff, who in 1941 was making his big league debut with the Chicago Cubs, actually believed that he had led the hitters in the Pacific Coast League the year before because his wife gave him the hotfoot. . . .

Young Don Hendrickson, then with the Yankees, refused to shave when he was going to pitch, and other players refused to take a bath during a run of good luck. Such a taboo on bathing led to decidedly uncomfortable days for the New York Giants in the thirties. After a bad losing streak, the Giants finally won a ball game, and on that same day the player responsible for the victory developed a case of itch. Luck and the itch were put together like 2 and 2, and the other players wouldn't let him take a bath or do anything else to relieve the ailment, although it was contagious.

After that the Giants kept winning day after day, and soon half the team were scratching and squirming. None of them dreamed of bathing or employing other anti-itch measures, however, until an opposing pitcher finally took them to the cleaners.

This willingness to suffer for one's superstition is not confined to players.

When P. K. Wrigley, owner of the Chicago Cubs then, attended a game, he never smoked till the Cubs came to bat. Then at the first pitch he would light up a cigarette and keep it going as long as the club was at bat. Sometimes during a sustained slugging rampage, the cigarette would get so short that it scorched his fingers, but he didn't seem to mind. The Cubs claimed that this helped them considerably.

10

LOOKA TH' LIL ANGEL

The selection of a bat boy, or a mascot, is hedged with black magic. When the Yankees hired a new mascot once more than a hundred boys were interviewed. At last a youngster named Timmy Sullivan was engaged because he could trace his ancestry right back to the O'Suhllhivaghu who was official minstrel and mascot to Brian Boru. The Yankees felt that blood would tell.

Birds, beasts, and even reptiles are often called upon to sway baseball's fickle divinities. The Phillies once made a ceremony of burying a rabbit which they swore brought Dizzy Dean luck when hurling against them. Lou Gehrig's mother used to provide her son and his Yankee teammates with pickled eels to keep them hitting.

The Cincinnati Reds once carried with them on all their travels a little dog named Cinci, just because the pooch had happened to wander into their clubhouse on a day when the tide of battle turned in their favor in the last half of the ninth.

And, yes, there is still another superstition that sways even such a sane and sensible person as Bob Feller. The big Iowan was scared to death of a little hole in the ground. He almost broke up a game in the Yankee Stadium because of a minute indentation in the pitcher's box. The crowd booed, and the wrathful umpires pleaded and threatened, but the mighty farmer just wouldn't pitch a lick until ground attendants came and filled up the hole.

"It wouldn't have been lucky," said Bob.

* * *

Bobo Newsom had a paper phobia. He refused to pitch if there was any paper around the mound or on the infield where he could see it. He held up games until it was cleaned up. Of course, other players drove him daffy by tearing up paper in small bits and scattering them around the mound. Newsom also had a habit of throwing the rosin bag over his right shoulder every time he handled it.

Dizzy Trout wouldn't pitch unless he had a big red bandanna handkerchief in his hip pocket.

Wes Ferrell was a student of astrology and wanted his "lucky days" by the stars for starting assignments.

Lew Burdette, of the Milwaukee Braves, always runs to the plate when it is his turn to bat.

Joe Adcock always bounces the ball high on the infield before the half inning commences.

Bill Tuttle, third baseman and center fielder for the Minnesota Twins, has always considered 13 his lucky number and he wears it on his uniform.

Most of the players on the team run for the same seat they occupied on previous charter flights, perhaps feeling that if they survived one flight they could do it again from the same seat.

* * *

H. L. Masin of *Scholastic Magazines* reported:
"You may not believe it, but many big league baseball games are won or lost by good luck charms, jinxes, black magic, and 101 other forms of abracadabra. In no other sport are there so many superstitious stars. Some of the

14

things they do are batty. They admit it. But they would no more stop doing them than take the field without their gloves.

"Our old-time players thought it was lucky to tip their hats to empty barrels, or stick chewing gum over their eyebrows before going to bat.

"Our stars today do things no less weird. Ducky Medwick, one-time Brooklyn Dodger, made a point of kicking third base when he came in from left field. Carl Hubbell, New York Giant, would rather jump off a cliff than step on the foul line when he walked to and from the bench.

"Belief in the power of certain clothes is another common superstition. The Cincinnati Reds feel they won the pennant in 1940 because of an old dirty tie owned by manager Bill McKechnie. He wore the magic tie day in and day out, and sometimes even slept in it. It was this, the players swear, that pulled them through the tight spots.

"Music, too, has its charms. After a big event, like clinching the pennant or winning the World Series, the New York Yankees always break into 'Roll Out the Barrel.' Lou Novikoff, the mad Russian of the Cubs, thinks 'My Wild Irish Rose' is the luckiest of songs. Once upon receiving a trophy, he stood at home plate and sang it to the fans.

"Bats are loaded with whammies. A bat is supposed to contain just so many singles, doubles, triples and homers. That's why a player so rarely lends his bat, even to a buddy. They are afraid this may take a hit out of the bat that they (the lenders) may need themselves."

* * *

Raymond Schuessler reported for the *American Mercury* in 1956:

15

"Superstition is good for a ballplayer," says Lefty O'Doul. "It has psychological effects. It keeps a player's mind revolving around baseball.

"Not that I think if I stepped on the foul line it really would lose a game, but it's just that it has become part of the game for me. 'Course I don't really believe stepping on the foul line would influence the game in the least . . ." he said, crossing his eyes, spinning three times in short hops while pulling his little fingers till they cracked, and spitting in his left rear pocket four times.

Most ballplayers today are superstitious. The doodles that batters draw in the batting box, the precise route they take to their positions, the ritual before and after each inning, are a whammies delight. Of course, they don't spit in a cross-eyed woman's beer any more or go back to the hotel to change their clothes if they pass a funeral.

John McGraw never ridiculed superstition. He even helped create a few to give his players confidence. One year his eccentric star, Mike Donlin, saw a truckload of empty barrels roll by the stadium. That day he got three big hits— and a new superstition was born. The next day he couldn't beg a base hit. "If I could only see a few empty barrels," wailed Mike. McGraw hired a wagon full of empty barrels to circle the stadium every day and Mike went crazy blasting hits all over the field. The Giants won the pennant.

Superstitions start in even crazier ways. When Al Simmons of the fabulous Philadelphia A's of the thirties went into a slump, he would wander about in a daze trying to figure out means of exorcising these imps of ill luck. One day he wandered out of the shower after a particularly disastrous day and as he stood dripping wet in front of his locker, he unconsciously put on his hat. Hysteria rocked the dressing room at the sight of the sopping, naked slugger posing de-

16

jectedly and blankly with nothing on but his hat. Al cracked not a smile, but dressed and stomped out of the dressing room. The next day, Al broke loose with four booming hits to win the game. Forever after Al would go through the same ritual: take a shower and then stand in front of his locker with nothing on but his hat. He continued to hit and the habit was taken up by the rest of the A's ballplayers and soon spread around the league.

When the Yankees of 1920 played in Boston, Joe Dugan always stopped in church to light a candle before every game. Waite Hoyt watched with envy while Joe went three for three in the first game. Next day Dugan again lit his candle and walloped two homers. On the third day Waite was scheduled to pitch, so he went to the same church and lit a candle. That afternoon he had his brains scrambled by a Boston rally. He called Joe aside.

"Joe, how come that when you light candles you get base hits by the bushelful and when I light a candle I get clobbered?"

"Simple," said Joe. "When you left the church the Boston gamblers came in and blew out your candle."

Amos Rusie, the Giants' old fireball, never entered a game until he had first played a game of "craps" with the club's handyman. Babe Ruth used to step on second base when coming in from right field, and if he ever neglected to do so, he would trot out from the dugout to perform his voodoo.

Stan Musial never will eat his breakfast any other way than one egg, two buckwheat cakes and then another egg. Bobo Newsom never would tie his own shoelaces on the day he was to pitch. He'd suit up and stand in the middle of the dressing room until somebody came over, knelt down and laced his boots.

17

Joe DiMaggio once began a hitting streak the night he took a Broadway chorus girl on a date. To him the leggy beauty became a symbol and he continued to date her. His hitting streak continued for two weeks and Joe dated the girl every night. Then one day Joe went hitless and the newspapers reported: "Miss . . . and DiMaggio have come to the parting of the ways."

Alvin Crowder, the big Washington pitcher, was in a terrible slump until he accidentally picked up Walter Johnson's glove. With it he pitched a superb game. Johnson never got his glove back. Crowder went on to win fifteen straight games with it. Then, one day he was called on to relieve. Cockily he dug his treasured glove out of his secret hiding place and strutted to the mound with high hopes of tying the league record of 16 straight wins, and maybe never losing a game the rest of his life. After a dozen base hits rattled off, Alvin drooped back to the dugout.

"Here!" he berated the startled Johnson. "Here's your damn unlucky glove! How can you use such a foul, jinxed-up contraption?"

Most of the superstition centers around the bat. All sorts of incantations are used in an attempt to inject greater efficacy. Boning, in which a bat is rubbed with a bone, did not originate through the logical principle of closing the pores of the wood to give a harder hitting surface, but as a method of instilling an attraction to horsehide—bone and skin, you know.

Before Harry Walker came up to the big leagues he got into the habit of only using a bat that had been used to stir dark stain in the bat factory. This came about after he had been in a slump. Hoping to order an old type of bat, he visited the factory and was told that the model no longer existed. However, one of his models was found. It was being used to stir a batch of dark stain. The bat was dried out and Walker won the Little World Series for Columbus against Louisville in 1941 with it.

One year Pepper Martin's batting average dropped off. He tried everything but couldn't snap out of it. Since ball-players in those days considered finding a hairpin an omen of a base hit, a sympathetic sports writer decided to bolster Pepper's confidence. He bought a boxful of pins and scattered them about the hotel from the elevator to the front door. Instead of Martin, however, Ducky Medwick hopped out of the elevator and fell to his knees to gobble up all the hairpins in sight. The sports writer implored, "Save a few for Martin, Ducky, he's got to break his slump."

"The hell with Martin; let him find his own base hits," growled Medwick who went on to hit .360 that season.

Everyone knew about Eddie Collins' habit of sticking a piece of chewing gum on the button of his cap when he went to bat. When he got two strikes he would take the gum off his cap and chew like blazes. One day Ted Lyons sprinkled red pepper on Eddie's gum before he went to bat. When the count went to two strikes, Collins tore the gum off his cap and started chewing. He spat—and struck out. "I'll fine the joker a million dollars if I find him," sputtered manager Collins.

The most famous of luck charms was the late Eddie Bennett, the hunchback who used to hang around the gate of the Polo Grounds when the Yankees played there. One day Happy Felsch, the Chicago outfielder, happened to see the hunchback there and gave his hump a playful rub. That afternoon the White Sox beat the Yankees. They swept the series and went on to belabor the Giants in the 1917 World Series. Bennett was made official mascot of the Chicago Club. Wherever Bennett moved he brought luck. When he went to Brooklyn in 1920 the Dodgers won the pennant. After he moved to the Yankees they ran away with the World Series in four straight games.

You hear the story about players wearing the same clothing while on a hitting streak. Maybe there's nothing to it, but Joe Green, former Philadelphia Athletics player, once went on a hitting streak which lasted for more than a month. Joe refused to change his suit. His wife finally couldn't bear the dirt and sent his suit to the cleaners. Next day, wearing a bright new suit, Joe broke his leg.

Here's what another uniform did to a Detroit team. A few years ago Art Houtteman wore No. 15. He started off by losing eight straight games, although he was pitching well. He happened to throw against Bob Lemon when Bob notched a no-hitter. He lost several 1-0 and 2-1 games. Hoping to break the jinx Houtteman made a deal. He traded his No. 15 uniform for George Kell's No. 21. Promptly a line drive fractured Kell's wrist. When he recovered from that, his jaw was broken by a bad bouncing ball. Now, Kell isn't superstitious, but he was through with uniform No. 15.

Houtteman didn't want the uniform back and the club promised him No. 10 once the season started. But for the time being Art would have to wear No. 15 again. He did and at the start of spring training he was almost killed in an auto accident. Of course, some superstitions have their practical value, such as the time Grover Cleveland Alexander used to warm up with a 12 pound shot a few times before pitching so that the ball would seem light in comparison. For a practical superstition you couldn't beat Germany Schmidt's habit of sneaking out to the ball park in the middle of the night before he was to pitch. He would dig up the pitcher's rubber and move it a foot or so closer to the plate.

II. The Believe-It-or-Nots in Baseball

A Collection of the Oddities That Happened on the Diamond

The major league infielder who played 339 games with a broken leg. Accidentally shot while hunting, Charley Gelbert's left leg had all but one tendon severed, fibula entirely disconnected and four inches of posterior artery and nerve entirely destroyed. The only support left in this area being the tibia and blood supply. X-rays showed about 2½ inches of fibula just hanging in leg, entirely disconnected. But in spite of this terrific handicap, Gelbert was back in the game and played in 100 games with the Toledo team in 1938. Gelbert was the St. Louis shortstop who was the hero of the 1930 World Series. After his comeback in 1935 he was selected by Philadelphia sports writers as the most courageous athlete in the country.

The accident occurred in the fall of 1932. He was in the hospital over two years, until January, 1935. Then started what baseball writers have termed the most courageous endeavor in the history of baseball. Charley began his comeback, playing 62 ball games with the Cardinals in 1935 and 90 ball games with the same club in 1936. In the fall of '36 he was traded to Cincinnati, where he played until July 10, 1937, when he was sent to Detroit. With these two clubs he played 87 games. He came to Toledo of the American Association in the spring of 1938.

Dan O'Leary, playing with Peoria in 1883, knocked a home run and ran the wrong way. He was declared out. He stands as the only man in organized baseball to make a home run the wrong way.

Port Huron is playing Peoria in 1883. It is the last half of the ninth, two out, score 7–7, O'Leary at bat. Twice he spins around like a dervish, fooled by the pitcher's deceptive drop. The twirler tempts fate once too often. A sharp crash of ash meeting horsehide tells of a ball smacked on the trademark. O'Leary has swung from his heels; he falls to his knees, loses his sense of direction, jumps up, and heads toward third base.

The crowd howls its astonishment. O'Leary takes the distant drumfire for applause. He rounds third, head down, looking to neither right nor left. He turns second, kicking up a cloud of dust, and digs out for first. Now he has skirted first base and is heading home, oblivious to the ravings of his teammates. He imagines the ball being relayed to the plate; he slides, spikes flashing toward the grinning catcher who gives him elbow room.

The umpire raises his arm, semaphore fashion, jerking a thumb in the direction of the bench. "You're out." "What for?" bellows O'Leary. "For running the wrong way around," says the heartless official.

22

Warren Rosar, backstop for the Philadelphia Athletics, caught 47 games without an error between September 15, 1945, and May 18, 1947.

On August 25, 1936, three Braves gained a rare feat in baseball: in a single inning they hit 2 doubles apiece.

Mel Ott, New York Giants great, scored 6 runs in a single game on August 4, 1934, and again in 1944. He walked 5 times in each of 4 games between 1929 and 1944.

The entire Cleveland team hit and scored in one inning on June 9, 1908, against Boston.

The Braves and the Cubs, in a double-header on May 30, 1956, hit 15 home runs. The Milwaukee Braves accounted for 9 of them.

Jim Konstanty, relief pitcher for the Phillies, worked in 74 games in the season of 1950.

In last place on July 11, 1914, the Boston Braves won the pennant, winning 59 of their last 75 games.

Connie Mack's Athletics played through two World Series without a substitution, not a relief pitcher, pinch hitter, or pinch runner.

"Old Hoss" Radbourn pitched 745 innings in 1884.

Miss Jackie Mitchell, girl pitcher, struck out Babe Ruth and Lou Gehrig on six pitched balls, April 2, 1931, in Chattanooga, Tennessee.

John Clancy, of the Chicago White Sox, went through a complete game at first base without handling a fielding chance in St. Louis.

Buck Weaver, of the Chicago White Sox, hit 17 fouls in succession for Chicago with Babe Ruth pitching for Boston.

Max Carey, former Pittsburgh star, stole 51 bases out of 53 attempts.

Charles McCoy, of Fort Worth, Texas, made 31 errors in one game in 1932.

Ty Cobb ran 99 miles as a base runner during his career.

Jimmy Johnston stole 124 bases in one season—the modern record. However, Johnston compiled this high mark with San Francisco in the Pacific Coast League where the season was long. Johnston played in 201 games. This prize-pilfering performance resulted in Johnston's going up to the major leagues, where he was a star for a number of years with Brooklyn. He later was manager of the Chattanooga club in the Southern League.

Duke Farrell threw out 8 players trying to steal—in one game.

Soveski of Stanford University pitched a no-hit game against the University of Southern California—but lost. March 29, 1929.

Ruth, greatest of all baseball players, performed this prodigious clouting feat in an exhibition game on Wrigley

Ripley's — Believe It or Not!

PHIL CAVARRETTA of the Chicago Cubs RETIRED FROM BASEBALL IN **1953** AFTER HAVING PLAYED IN EXACTLY **1953** GAMES

GOODLOE ROGERS a semi-pro catcher *MADE AN UNASSISTED TRIPLE PLAY* –Pontiac, Mich.

JAMES HILL of Fort Wayne, Ind. HAS NO LEGS *YET HE PLAYS BASEBALL!*

BABE RUTH USED **170** BATS EACH SEASON BILL TERRY NEEDED ONLY **2** BATS TO LEAD THE NATIONAL LEAGUE'S HITTERS IN 1930

Field, Los Angeles, in February, 1927. Babe, who always aimed to please, stood at the plate for an hour while several pitchers tossed balls at him which he walloped over the fence—125 in all.

Lefty Grove, of Baltimore, struck out 68 men in 45 innings in 1925.

Babe Herman tripled with the bases full and a double play resulted. He overran the two base runners ahead of him.

Ferdie Schupp allowed less than one earned run a game in the 1916 season.

Babe Ruth hit 5 home runs in 6 times up.

Jimmy Dykes, of the Philadelphia Athletics, made 5 hits on 5 pitched balls in 1927.

Hack Wilson fanned 6 times in succession.

Only one baseball was used in a complete nine-inning game between Chicago and Cincinnati.

The Niagara baseball club of Buffalo, New York, scored 209 runs in a single game.

J. Wadsworth gave up 36 hits to Philadelphia in one game.

During the 1906 baseball season the New York Yankees played 5 double-headers on 5 consecutive playing days. Their opponents were the Washington Senators for 3 double-headers, then the Philadelphia Athletics and finally the Boston Red Sox.

Max Surkont of the Milwaukee Braves struck out 8 men in a row on May 25, 1953, at the expense of the Cincinnati Reds.

Eddie Collins stole 6 bases in a single game on September 11, 1912, while playing against Detroit. Collins was the great American League second baseman for the Philadelphia Athletics. Eleven days later he did it again, this time against the St. Louis Browns.

Grover Cleveland Alexander, the pitching world-beater for the Philadelphia Nationals, in the 1916 season pitched 16 shutouts in gaining 33 victories.

Tony Lazzeri, the all-time great second baseman for the New York Yankees, hit two home runs with the bases full in a single game on May 24, 1936.

John D. Chesbro in 1904 and playing for the New York Yankees, known then as the Highlanders, won 41 games out of 53 pitched by him that year.

Joe Schipo of the Tampa, Florida, ball club, hit two homers with bases full in the same inning.

Larry Doyle won the national batting championship with an average of only .320 in 1915.

Stuffy McGinnis played 154 games without committing an error.

Babe Ruth walked 171 times in one season.

"Home Run" North made 9 home runs in one game in 1868.

James Hinson, of Monroe, North Carolina, made 16 hits in succession as a pinch hitter in 1923.

Josh Devore, of the New York Giants, stole 4 bases in one inning in 1912. He was up twice.

Famous iron man Joe McGinnity when 52 years old pitched and won 4 games in 11 days, scoring a shutout in the last one.

Babe Ruth hit 714 home runs during his career in the big leagues.

Walter Johnson, of the Washington Senators, pitched 56 scoreless innings in succession in 1913.

Virgil Trucks, the strikeout king, fanned 451 hitters in 299 innings, at Andalusia, Alabama, in the Florida League in 1938.

Sam Crawford, of the Detroit Tigers, led the American League with 7 home runs in 1908.

Abner Doubleday, the reputed father of baseball, fired the first Union shot of the Civil War. As captain he fired the first shot from Fort Sumter in reply to the Confederate bombardment in Charleston in 1861.

Charlie Gehringer, of Detroit, hit a single, double, triple, and home run in that order in a game between Detroit and St. Louis on May 27, 1939.

A baseball game was delayed on account of hot weather and two hours later was called off, this time because of a snowstorm in Gallup, New Mexico, on July 4, 1933.

In 1906 the Chicago Cubs won 116 games for an all-time record, losing only 36.

Frank Chance, first baseman for the Chicago Cubs, while playing in a game on May 30, 1904, made a unique record. He was hit by a pitched ball five times.

The all-time major league record for a single game was attained by Johnny Burnett, shortstop for the Cleveland Indians, when he got 9 hits on July 10, 1932, in a wildly played contest against the Athletics.

Baseball's Hall of Famer Cy Young pitched more than nine hundred big league baseball games from 1890 to 1911. His total was nine hundred and six games and he won 511 in all.

Under the shadow of Walter Johnson, the strikeout king, Bob Feller proved himself in 1946 by striking out 348 men.

Elmer Smith, playing right field for the Cleveland Indians, hit 7 consecutive extra-base hits—4 home runs and 3 doubles—during the 1921 season.

On May 1, 1920, the Brooklyn Dodgers played the Boston club a 26-inning 1–1 game, and the umpires were forced to call it a no-decision bout on account of fast-falling darkness.

First baseman Alex Hooks played a complete 10-inning game without having a ball thrown to him at first. Fort Worth, Texas, June 21, 1942.

Babe Ruth won more prizes at golf than in baseball.

31

Al Reach, of the Philadelphia Athletics, scored 34 runs in one day in 1865.

Miller Huggins, playing second base for St. Paul, accepted 19 chances in 9 innings in 1902.

James Galvin, of St. Louis, Missouri, who pitched 4 no-hit big league games from 1876 to 1884, weighed 300 pounds.

Joe Wood started in pro baseball by pitching for the Boston Bloomer Girls.

The Portland, Oregon, baseball club played 88 consecutive innings without allowing a single run in the Pacific Coast League in 1910.

Dixie Walker hit a home run and caught the ball himself. The ball remained lodged in the right-field screen until Walker shook it loose and caught it at Ebbets Field in 1949.

Ed Delahanty was the only player who led both the National and the American Leagues in batting: .408 at Philadelphia in the National League in 1899 and .376 at Washington in the American League in 1902.

Louis ("Bobo") Newsom, of the St. Louis Browns, pitching in both games of a double-header, walked the first four men in one game and then started the second game by striking out the same four players.

Ray Hayworth, Detroit catcher, played 100 games without an error.

Harry Hulen, of Minneapolis, was at bat 6 times, walked 6 times, and scored 6 times on August 1, 1894.

Joe Cronin, of the Boston Red Sox, pinch-hit two home runs on the same afternoon, against the Athletics.

Lou Gehrig, star first baseman for the New York Yankees, hit four consecutive home runs in a game on June 3, 1932. Larrupin' Lou hit 23 home runs with the bases full during his career.

Bill Wambsganss, Cleveland Indians' second sacker, made an unassisted triple play in a World Series game against the Brooklyn Dodgers on October 10, 1920.

Jimmy Foxx, the Red Sox slugger, walked 6 times in a single game on June 16, 1938.

A great performance was the pitching of two consecutive no-hit no-run games by Johnny Vander Meer, of the Cincinnati Reds. On June 10, 1938, he pitched against the Boston Bees and retired his opponents with only 28 men facing him. Five days later Vander Meer pitched against the Brooklyn Dodgers and allowed only 8 men to reach first base, all on walks.

In a single wild game on August 25, 1922, the Chicago Cubs and the Philadelphia Phillies scored 49 runs. The Cubs lost 26–23.

In 1905 the World Series went five games and every game was a shutout. With the famous Christy Mathewson pitching, the Giants won the series.

On April 15, 1911, Walter Johnson, pitching for the Washington Senators, fanned four batters in a single inning. One man reached first base when the catcher dropped the ball.

Phil Cavarretta, of the Chicago Cubs, retired from baseball in 1953 after having played in exactly 1,953 games.

Eddie Yost, of the Washington Senators, in one time at bat hit 13 consecutive foul balls.

The umpire of the first baseball game played in Berlin, Germany, wore a suit of armor, on June 12, 1912.

Babe Ruth, holder of 34 regular season records and 26 World Series records, never received the most valuable player award.

A baseball hit 400 feet has twice as much destructive energy as a bullet fired from a 38-caliber pistol.

Ty Cobb made 5 hits in one game 5 times in one season.

Rube Marquard, the Giants' star pitcher, won 19 straight victories in 1913. He beat every club in the league, and Boston and Philadelphia 4 times each.

In 1957 the Baltimore Orioles played 80 games without an error, a new major league record.

The Milwaukee slugger Joe Adcock, playing against the Dodgers on July 31, 1954, got 5 extra-base hits in one game.

During the summer of 1941 Joe DiMaggio hit safely in 56 straight games.

In 1913 Christy Mathewson did not give a base on balls in 68 consecutive innings.

35

On September 16, 1924, first baseman Jim Bottomley of the St. Louis Cardinals drove in 12 runs in a single game with 6 hits.

The Yankees played 308 games without being once shut out from August 2, 1931, to August 3, 1933.

Jim Hegan, of the Cleveland Indians, caught three no-hitters: by Don Black in 1947, by Bob Lemon in 1948, and by Bob Feller in 1951.

The Giants have won the most National League pennants while in New York, 15 in all, including the four in a row won under John J. McGraw in 1921–1924.

In the 41 years since their first victory, the New York Yankees have captured 26 flags. Included in this is a record string of five in a row under Casey Stengel in 1949–1953.

Ty Cobb led the American League 12 times in batting. Honus Wagner led the National League 8 times.

Sandy Koufax, of the Dodgers, broke a 58-year record of the National League by fanning 269 batters in 1961, breaking Christy Mathewson's record of 267 set back in 1903.

Hub Pruett, pitcher for the St. Louis Browns, was Babe Ruth's jinx. He struck out the Bambino 19 out of 31 times.

In 1953 Yankee home run slugger Mickey Mantle slammed a 565-foot home run, thus establishing a record.

D. H.

III. Anecdotage

Uncle Robbie and Others

BY GARRY SCHUMACHER

The day games in St. Louis in the late twenties and early thirties were always wearing. The Cardinals were tough to beat, and it was always hot. It was my experience with the Dodgers that whenever they got to St. Louis the most important guy with the troupe was the club doctor; for one reason or another there would be three or four players who suddenly came up with ailments or injuries that were an excuse not to play. This time Glenn Wright had a stiff neck, Wally Gilbert had a sprained ankle, Gordon Slade a hangnail, and there were a couple of other absentees. When the time came to take the field Uncle Robbie had to put together a makeshift infield, which installed Fresco Thompson at third base, a position he had never played before. To complicate the situation, "Chick" Hafey was probably the best right-handed pull hitter of the time, and the soft ball throwing—I always thought he released the ball with a pulse beat—Joe Shaute, was the Dodger pitcher.

Well, the first time up, Hafey whistled a line drive down

37

the line that cracked Thompson on the kneecap, played a couple of bars of "Yankee Doodle" as it ricocheted from one shin to the other, and finally sifted through into left field for a double.

The next time Hafey came to bat you couldn't tell who was playing left field, Thompson or Lefty O'Doul. Taking in the situation at a glance, Hafey proceeded to drop down a bunt, and walked to first base with another base hit.

Nothing much was said when the Dodgers came back to the bench until Thompson beckoned to the bat boy.

"Sonny," he asked, "have you got a dime?" When assured that the youngster had, Thompson said, "Go out to the concession stand and buy an ice cream cone, preferably strawberry. Then, when the Cardinals come back from the field, give it to Chick Hafey with my compliments.

"And be sure and tell him, that if he bunts again he will get another one."

Most of Dizzy Dean's games against the Giants had something to offer in the way of writing material.

In this one, also at St. Louis, Dizzy had an easy game for a change (Carl Hubbell used to beat him whenever they met) and was winning by a 7 or 8 to 1 score when the Giants came to bat in the eighth.

With us at the time, at second base, was Burgess Whitehead, who had been a particular pal and buddy of Dizzy's while they were together on the Cardinals. Diz liked Burgess very much, and whenever the circumstances allowed he wouldn't make it too tough for him to get a hit. Burgess was a good high ball, fast ball hitter, so the fit was perfect.

This time Burgess crashed the fat fast ball gift, and the first thing the ball hit was Dizzy Dean's head. It caromed off his noggin so hard it sailed on a high parabola out into

38

left field, where finally Joe Medwick ran it down as a two-base hit.

Diz was flattened by the wallop, and to be honest we thought he was dead. He never moved a muscle or flicked an eyelash. Presently they lugged him off on a stretcher, and Jim Dawson and I thought it behooved us to go to the dressing room to see how badly he was hurt.

When we got there Dizzy was lying on the rubbing table, while brother Paul fanned him with a towel. Finally Dizzy came to, and when he recognized his brother, his first words were:

"There ain't going to be a knot thar, is there?"

"Don't you worry," Paul soothed. "It didn't hit you but a glancing blow."

The Uncle Robbie stories are without number, of course, but I don't ever remember reading this one in print.

It came up, as I remember it, in 1931, when the Dodgers were pretty good, and had a chance to win it all until a slump in late September.

But in early June they were up there, and had a series with the Cardinals at Ebbets Field. Just before the first game began, Robbie suddenly remembered that he had just traded Jake Flowers from the Dodgers to the Cardinals.

"Say, he'll know all our signs, won't he?" Robbie inquired of nobody in particular. "We'll have to change them before we start the game."

Immediately there were a dozen suggestions advanced.

"Here's a set McGraw used to use," Lefty O'Doul volunteered.

Jack Quinn had another idea. "This is one of the best sets Connie Mack ever used," he urged strongly.

The round table conference to discuss all these suggestions had reached no decision when it came time to play. The upshot of it was that the Dodgers went into action with no signs.

Johnny Frederick was the first hitter. The count got to 2 and 0 when Robbie wanted to flash a hit sign. He had to sit idly by as Frederick took it for a strike.

"Oooh, a home run ball!" Robbie moaned. Now it came down to 3 and 1, and for some reason Robbie thought it time to flash a "take" sign. Instead, Frederick took a swipe at the pitch and whaled it over the fence.

That pacified Robbie for a while, and he didn't worry about the signs for the rest of the afternooon. Even the next day he didn't press the matter, and the Dodgers won again. In fact, they went off on a ten-game winning streak that took them into the lead.

By now the Dodgers were in Chicago, and Robbie called another meeting.

"It's been fun," he allowed, "but we're carrying this thing too far. Here we are in first place, and who ever heard of a team winning a pennant without signs? It just isn't dignified."

You've guessed the rest. The Dodgers finally adopted a set of signs, lost that afternoon to the Cubs and went into a tail spin. They never did get into first place again.

With the old Dodgers, Babe Herman was Uncle Robbie's fair-haired boy; so far as Robbie was concerned Babe could do no wrong. On the other hand, Hollis Thurston, with his caustic tongue and sharp wit, raised Robbie's hackles every now and again. (Besides, Sloppy's pitching repertoire didn't include a high hard one.)

On this particular afternoon, at Ebbets Field, Hollis was in the bullpen, which in Brooklyn was located against the

40

FRACTURED ROOKIE

and then they started curving him....

41

grandstand railing in right field. Getting the sun with him was Paul Richards, at that time one of the extra catchers.

It went along an easy game with the Cubs, with the Dodgers winning by a big score. The only interruption occurred in the top of the eighth, when Kiki Cuyler looped a fly into right field, close to the foul line. Either Herman didn't see the ball hit or lost it in the sun, because he never stirred until the ball plopped down onto the field, a couple of feet fair. Before Babe retrieved it Cuyler had a triple, but nothing untoward developed since the next Cub was the third out.

Out in the bullpen, Thurston said to Richards:

"Let's walk back to the bench, and see how Babe gets out of this one."

Babe got to the bench about the same time they did but Robbie had words only for the bullpen twins.

"What are you guys doing out there in the bullpen?" Robbie demanded. "Sleeping? Why didn't you holler and tell Babe that was going to be a fair ball?"

Pirate Memories

BY CHET SMITH

My first tangible experience with the Pirates came in the 1920's, but my first tangle with Barney Dreyfuss was not to come until the early 1930's. Barney was one of the most remarkable men I have ever met. With a couple of helpers in the office and a scout or two he kept building contenders, largely on his own good judgment. Contrary to belief, he was not a stingy man. He paid good salaries and in the old days any player who cared to could let Barney take a certain amount of his money and invest it in the market. He played the horses heavily. Barney guaranteed the player all profits and if there was a loss he would return the original stake. Several of the players got a good chunk on the side that way.

At the time I am speaking about, our editor got the idea of proposing that the Pirates institute a Ladies' Day—a new wrinkle at that time. I visited Barney and put it up to him. He listened me out and then, in his high-pitched, accented voice, he gave me his answer.

"No! When the boys went away to war the ladies took their jobs and wouldn't give them back. They can pay to get in my ball park."

There was no Ladies' Day at Forbes Field until after Barney died.

Frank Frisch was undoubtedly our best copy. One summer, a dignified old gaffer who had a box seat directly behind third base, where Frank coached, began to ride him unmercifully. Frisch put up with it for a long time and then one day walked over and formally introduced himself.

"My name is Frisch," he said, behind a dead pan. "What is your name?" The gent, taken aback, told him. "And what do you do?" Frank persisted. It turned out the old man was the head of a major concern downtown.

"Are you going to be in your office tomorrow?" Frank asked. The man said he was.

"Okay," Frank said. "We have the day off and I'll be down to tell you how to run *your* business."

The guy was a good sport. He invited Frank to make it a luncheon date and they wound up good friends.

There are a million Paul Waner stories, but the best one happened in Chicago. Paul had been out on the town the

44

night before. It was one of Chicago's beastly hot days and Paul obviously was not in good shape when he turned up at the park. First three times up he didn't come within a foot of the ball. Fourth time, eighth inning, Pirates behind by a run, two men on. Paul lined the first pitch against the ivy in right field. Two runs scored, Paul slid into third in a cloud of dust for a triple. As he did, Charlie Grimm, then the Cubs' manager, leaped out of the dugout.

"Goddammit!" Charlie yelled. "You would sober up now!"

Like all clubs, the Pirates were hard put to it to find a respectable quorum during the World War II years. One of their finds was a young outfielder from Harrisburg. He was a dead ringer for Ted Williams, but there the resemblance ended.

The club, when it sent out contracts in those days, told the players that if they wished it would hold out a certain amount from the pay checks and buy war bonds. The young man replied to this offer:

"I do not need a war bond. I have one."

I was working for Bill Peet my first year in sports. The Dodgers were in town. Bill sent me out to the Schenley to ask Robbie the name of his pitcher for the next day's game. In those days pitching selections weren't announced routinely as they are now.

It was a hot night. I found Robbie sitting out on the lawn with a bunch of his players. I introduced myself and asked the question.

Robbie thought a minute, scratched his head and said, finally, "Guess it will be Daz, over there"—pointing to Vance.

"Hell, Robbie," Daz grumbled, "I pitched today."

47

There was a short silence, then Robbie spoke up:
"Dammit, you just can't keep track a what's goin' on with
this ball club!"

The Great Waddell

BY GEORGE A. BARTON

This is the saga of George Edward ("Rube") Waddell,
one of the greatest left-handed pitchers in major league
annals, and likewise one of the most colorful and eccentric
characters our national pastime ever produced.

Several years before his death Connie Mack, the famous
owner and manager of the Philadelphia Athletics, visited in
Minneapolis with his lifelong friend, Mike Kelley, owner of
the Minneapolis Millers of the American Association.

During an interview with Mr. Mack, as all members of
the Athletics almost reverently referred to their boss, I asked
him innumerable questions about players of the past and
present. Among other queries, how he rated Rube Waddell
among left-handed pitchers.

"I have seen all of the best left-handers since the late
nineties," replied Mr. Mack, "but none was greater than
Waddell.

"Rube was gifted with blinding speed, a sharp breaking
curve, and superb control," continued Mr. Mack.

"He was a peculiar fellow, as you perhaps know. Rube
pitched for me for six years: 1902-03-04-05-06-07; consequently, I had ample time to become thoroughly conversant
with his ability.

"Although Rube was a giant of a fellow, standing 6 feet
1 inch and weighing in excess of 200 pounds, he unfor-
tunately possessed the mentality and irresponsibility of a lad

48

of sixteen. Time and again, he would shut out a rival team with a couple of hits and strike out ten or twelve batters, then desert our club. He would go fishing or hunting, as the spirit moved him. On other occasions, he would join a fire department; join a circus, or worse yet, would take a bartending job. It usually required much persuasion to coax him into rejoining our club.

"Despite his frequent absences from the club, Waddell pitched 46 games for me in 1904 and repeated that record in 1905; 41 games in 1906 and 43 games in 1907. His best performances for me were 23 wins and 7 losses in 1902; 22 and 16 in 1903; 25 and 19 in 1904 and 26 and 11 in 1905.

"For many years Waddell held the American League strikeout record with 16, which he set in 1902 and stood until Bobby Feller bettered it with 18 almost 40 years later.

"There is no telling of the records Rube would have set for winning games and striking out batters had he possessed the clean living habits of a Bobby Feller, Walter Johnson, or Christy Mathewson. Rube, you perhaps know, was a heavy drinker."

Now that you readers have been properly introduced by Connie Mack to the idiosyncrasies of the great Waddell, I will tell one of the funny stunts he pulled while pitching for the Minneapolis club of the American Association in 1910-'11-'12 during which he contributed yeoman service in the winning of three consecutive pennants.

Joe Cantillon, colorful manager of the Washington Senators in 1907-'08-'09, was part owner with his brother, Mike, and manager of the Millers during those years and through 1923 as a matter of fact.

In 1910, the Minneapolis team was engaged in a hot two-club pennant fight with the Louisville Colonels.

Following the winning of a double-header by the Millers

from Kansas City one hot Sunday afternoon in July, I visited the Minneapolis team's clubhouse to seek Cantillon's pitching choice for the opening game of a four-game series with the Toledo Mud Hens on Monday.

As Waddell was toweling himself dry after a shower, I heard Cantillon address Rube as follows:

"Listen, Rube," said Cantillon. "We're opening a four-game series with Toledo tomorrow. We've got to win this series, or we may be beaten out of the pennant by Louisville.

"You've gotta lay off the liquor for the next four days because I'm banking on you to win two of those games for us.

"You'll be pitching against Earl Yingling at least once, and maybe twice. I want you to be at your best to take care of Yingling and this Toledo outfit." (Editor's note: Yingling also was a corking good left-handed pitcher who later saw service with Cleveland, Brooklyn, Cincinnati, and Washington.)

"Okay, Joe," replied Waddell. "I'll take good care of Yingling and his Toledo pals."

Came Monday and the opener of the Millers-Mud Hens series. Neither Waddell nor Yingling put in an appearance at old Nicollet Park, home of the Millers in those days. The games of Tuesday, Wednesday, and Thursday were played with Waddell and Yingling still absent from the park. Fortunately, the Millers won three of the four games and increased their lead over Louisville.

Came Friday with the Millers scheduled to play a doubleheader against the Kansas City Blues.

With the first game starting at 1:30 P.M., I arrived at the park at 12:45. While visiting with manager Cantillon in front of the Millers' clubhouse, Waddell strolled onto the field carrying a string of fish, and was greeted by an ex-

50

plosion of uncomplimentary remarks by the riled Miller manager.

"Where the hell have you been?" Cantillon demanded.

"Now, now, Joe, don't get mad," replied Waddell. "You asked me to take care of Yingling, didn't you?"

"Yeah," replied Cantillon, "but what's that got to do with your not showing up to pitch?"

"Well, Yingling didn't show up either, did he, Joe?" replied Waddell, with an injured expression on his face.

"Come to think about it, Yingling didn't, but what about it?" was Cantillon's rejoinder.

"I made sure Yingling wouldn't beat me and our club by taking him fishing at Lake Minnetonka for four days," said Waddell.

Before Cantillon could reply, Rube said: "Look, Joe, today is Friday and I know you're a Catholic, so I brought this nice mess of fish for your dinner tonight. I hope you won't stay mad at me."

"Well, okay this time, Rube, but no more shenanigans like this," replied Cantillon, who, like most Irish, was quick to forgive and forget.

"Now, get into your uniform because you're going to pitch the first game of the double-header today." Waddell got himself back into Cantillon's good graces by defeating Kansas City, 3–1, with five hits.

Everything was serene between Joe and Rube for a week until *Cantillon received a bill for the fish from a meat market located only several blocks from Nicollet Park.*

Ten days later Minneapolis engaged in an important double-header with its closest rival, Louisville, in the Colonels' bailiwick.

It was a steaming hot July day in Louisville with the temperature in the 90's and humid as all getout.

Waddell pitched the first game and shut out the Colonels, 2–0, with six hits and fanning 12 batters.

As Rube rested in the Millers' dugout, Cantillon patted him on the back and said: "You sure looked great out there today, Rube—good enough to be back in the big leagues where you really belong. I'll bet you could beat the Colonels in the second game, Rube, so how about it?"

"Nix, Joe, nix," Rube replied. "It's too damned hot. Besides, I'm too damned tired."

Cantillon continued to pester Waddell to pitch the nightcap, whereupon Rube finally blurted: "Okay, Joe, I'll pitch the second game if you'll get me a bottle of whiskey."

"I'll have it for you right after the game, Rube," said Cantillon.

"Nix on that after the game stuff, Joe. I want it right now to help pep me up to pitch," retorted Rube.

Cantillon finally was compelled to grant Waddell's demand and sent the Millers' secretary to a nearby saloon for a quart of whiskey.

After a couple of hefty snorts, Waddell started the second game, which he also won by a score of 3–1, fanning 12 Louisville batters along the way. Between innings Rube finished off the quart of whiskey.

Waddell contracted tuberculosis early in the season of 1913, so Joe and Mike Cantillon gave him money to go to a sanitarium near San Antonio, Texas. He died April 1, 1914, and was buried in a cemetery in San Antonio, his grave marked only by a wooden shaft.

Harry J. Benson, president of the San Antonio baseball club of the Texas League, discovered the shabbily marked grave. Benson enlisted the aid of Connie Mack, John McGraw, and the Cantillon brothers—Joe and Mike. Benson raised $500, with the result that a beautiful tombstone, suitably inscribed, was placed on the last resting place of the great pitcher.

A Scoop for the Engineer

BY JOE WILLIAMS

On October 7, 1934, a big story broke. Babe Ruth announced that he was quitting the Yankees. This disclosure was made not at a massive press conference, as you'd have every right to assume, but to a guy he'd never seen before in his life.

It was, in fact, made to the engineer of a train which within minutes would be pulling out of St. Louis, headed for Detroit and the finale of the World Series. This may be the only milestone of the Babe's fabulous history from which an important detail is missing . . . the name of the engineer who got the big story first and firsthand.

I was the first sports writer to break the story in print, but I had got it on the rebound. The Babe and I were longtime friends, so I was not surprised when he requisitioned my compartment as a drop for a large quantity of barbecued ribs and beer which at his request had been delivered earlier to the train.

The Babe had a boyish curiosity about locomotives. So here we were, the two of us, idly inspecting the complicated conformation of this panting iron horse. It was, of course, impossible to mistake the Babe. The engineer recognized him instantly.

"How many home runs you going to hit for the Yankees next year?" the Great Unknown asked pleasantly.

"Hell with the Yankees," the Babe snorted. "I wouldn't

53

play with them again if they gave me the Stadium. I'm quitting."

"You mean you're quitting baseball?" the engineer pressed, incredulous.

"I mean—"

The familiar cry of "All aboard" abruptly ended the colloquy between the engineer, perhaps never to be identified, and the baseball hero who needed identification nowhere in the world.

The two of us, alone in the compartment, demolished ribs and beer all the way to Detroit or, more truthfully, until overcome by stuporous sleep.

(Meanwhile, I had arranged with Dan Daniel, our baseball writer, to file a piece en route to our paper, the New York *World-Telegram*.)

The Babe was understandably late getting to the park the next day. The press box was in tumult. The wire services had picked up the story, and the Detroit *News* gave it a page one play. Christy Walsh, the Babe's business representative, told sports writers seeking confirmation, or at least information, that he knew nothing about it . . . which was true. Also, he couldn't tell them where the Babe was. Last Walsh had seen of him was in the press box in St. Louis the day before.

The game was well under way by the time the Babe, perspiring copiously and looking only slightly less defunct than your correspondent, tumbled into his seat in the Briggs Stadium press box, where he immediately faced a barrage of questions.

Finally, in desperation, the Babe yelled for Walsh. "Get these guys off'n my back!"

The Babe had even scooped his own paper. He was covering the World Series for the New York *Journal-American*, among others.

Funny is not the word for this incident. Incredible would be closer. More like the Babe too. For there was little about George Herman Ruth's baseball life that wasn't incredible.

Of Babe and Izzy

I never saw Babe Ruth make a mistake on the diamond but off the field he wasn't infallible. I have in mind my first interview with him. That was back in the late fall of 1920, when I was sports editor of the Waterbury *American* and Ruth, having completed his first season with the Yankees, and topped it off with a barnstorming tour of Cuba, dropped into town to visit an automobile tire dealer who had been his buddy when both lived in Boston.

Fresh on the sports beat after being switched from the city staff, I had been reading about the difficulties the touring big-leaguers had had in Cuba because of the poor condition of the playing fields down there in those days. This, I thought, would be a good angle to pin my interview on, as several players on the trip had suffered leg injuries and the Yankees had made up their minds not to let their star take such chances again.

Having asked Babe a number of the usual banal questions, I switched suddenly to the one I hoped would win me the Pulitzer Prize. "Mr. Ruth," I said respectfully, "tell me this: What kind of diamonds do they have down in Cuba?"

Babe, his chair tilted back against the wall, knocked the ashes off the end of his cigar, gave the question a moment's

55

thought, and replied: "You can get some real good buys down there."

That, of course, was several years before Babe, sitting in the Yankee dugout at Miller Huggins Field at St. Petersburg during spring training, watching the antics of a rookie outfielder, who seemed to be enjoying a perpendicular snooze, turned to me and chortled: "Look at that guy out there in left field. He's in a transom!"

One of the most likable characters who ever covered the spring training camps was Izzy Kaplan, now, more is the pity, deceased. Everyone in baseball knew Izzy and liked him. Wherever he was, there laughter was unconfined. He could keep an Egyptian mummy in stitches. Born in Russia, he came to the United States early in the century, two hops ahead of a czarist pogrom. Almost immediately he landed a job with a newspaper as a photographer, that having been his trade back home in Ekaterinoslav. His first assignment was to go to the Polo Grounds (or Polish Grounds, as he always referred to the Giants' park thereafter) and cover a ball game. His introduction to baseball, which he didn't know from the kazotsky, was hilarious as he used to tell it in later years when he had learned to speak English like an uptown Yankee Doodle Boy—but with the remnants of a delightful Slobokka accent.

Some thirty-five years later, when Izzy could speak knowingly about a slider and a duster, he met one of the Hillerichs who own the Louisville Slugger bat factory, at spring training camp in St. Petersburg. Mr. Hillerich had some of his family with him and asked Kaplan to take photographs of them at the practice field. Ever obliging, Izzy not only took a number of shots of the Hillerich family but graciously developed the films, printed them on cabinet photo stock and had them mounted attractively, all at his own expense.

Mr. Hillerich was so pleased with this characteristic gesture on Izzy's part that he asked the photographer to give him the names of some of his friends and relatives to whom he wanted some bats sent. Izzy, who had his own special pronunciation of words and thought Mr. Hillerich gave the same sound value to them, made out a list that included his sister, her two children, himself and, since I was his assignment editor, me. He not only put down the address after the name but also the height and weight of each person. Then he proceeded to forget about the whole matter.

Some weeks later, when he had returned to New York, Izzy came to my cubicle one day and asked if I had received the bats Mr. Hillerich had promised.

"Yes," I told him, "and they are beautiful. They make a wonderful souvenir to hang on the walls of a den. Did you like yours?"

"Yes," said Izzy. "But I was a leedle disahpernted."

"But why?" I asked.

"Vell," he answered, "ven I gave him de sizes, all de time I t'ought he vas going to send us bats you sleep in!"

Babe

BY GENE WARD

Over on the right-hand side of the road, coming in from the airport, there's a group of buildings which, each year, brings back a rush of memory to this traveler. It is the St. Mary's Industrial School, where, a long time ago, a spindly-legged youngster from a broken family was reared and provided with the necessary prerequisites of manhood.

It is a little game I play as I pass by, this attempt at conjuring up in my mind's eye a picture of the lad as he was then. No doubt there have been a lot of changes since the boy who came to be known the world over as the Babe cavorted in these courtyards. Certainly there have been changes in the game he did so much to establish, many of them changes for the worse and threatening the whole foundation of a sport which once proudly bore the title of "our national pastime."

As I pass by this place where Babe Ruth got his start in life I can't help but feel that much of the answer to baseball's problem can be found here amid the beginnings of the man who was to be such a vital force in the game. Take the component parts of that force: the compassion of the Xaverian brothers who took the time to rear a boy with a zero potential; the man-hours of love's labor they sweated away on one lone, befuddled youngster.

What was done here bore tremendous fruit in the man the whole world came to know with affection and adulation. What was done here gave him a wonderful humanness; an amazing affinity for his fellow men. And the one thing that baseball seems to be fresh out of these days is players that come shining through with a special kind of glow.

Check down through today's major league rosters. There are the great ones like Williams and Musial, and some cut to a lesser measure like Mays and Mantle. But for all their sterling qualities as ballplayers none has that certain warmth of heart that comes shining through.

Not even DiMaggio, superb as he was, had it, and perhaps it is asking too much to expect this quality, even in smaller degree, in the modern big-league star. Perhaps in

58

this respect the mold was broken with the Babe. I hope not, because it is this warmth that is baseball's greatest lack today.

I basked in the Babe's special blend of humanness as a hicktown kid. Later I felt it as a young bleacherite in Yankee Stadium and it still was strong the day I saw him on the steps of the hospital as he came out that last time. But it was strongest of all that first meeting, and I still can see the Babe sitting in the tonneau of the old Pierce-Arrow, an ear-to-ear grin beaming from his brick-red face. The touring Yankees had just finished an exhibition hosing of my hometown heroes up in Oneonta, New York, and the Babe had unloaded one with the bases full.

There was a catcher named Sinstack who played for my team, and he was my most particular idol. Only on that afternoon he'd been shown up for what he was, a minor leaguer, and the denouement was sitting hard when Dad finally shepherded me out of Neahwa Park.

As we came out through the gate there sat the Babe and, thinking to perk up his deflated son, Dad led me over to the car.

"Babe," he said, "I'd like my son, Junior, to meet you," and with that the Babe stuck out his hamlike mitt. But not Junior. Bitter at the demise of his favorites and the spectacular bust of his particular hero, Junior kept his little hands clenched resolutely behind his back.

With that wonderful perception of his concerning kids, the Babe immediately sensed what was wrong with this silent small fry, and called after my slightly humiliated father, "Tell the boy we were lucky today," or some such kindness.

Years later, at the Westchester Country Club, he remem-

59

bered the incident, not the where or the who, but just the fact that once in his career a small boy had refused to shake his hand.

Life with Father

BY BILL SLOCUM

A couple of years ago a *Reader's Digest* editor suggested I do a story on my father for the magazine's "Greatest Man I Ever Knew" series, or whatever it was called.

Seemed like a fine idea. The man certainly fitted the title and the money from Pleasantville is always real good. So, I tried. And quit.

I didn't think anybody would believe my story. He sounded just a little too good to be true.

Now it's different. I know that so many people knew my father and while they cannot be expected to see him with the love and respect I hold I'm sure that they will agree in general with my estimate of an extraordinary human being.

Of course, his greatest trait was his kindness. He was wounded often because he wounded so easily but I don't think he ever wounded back. He had been taught to turn the other cheek and he did. Literally, in the case of Ed Barrow, who punched him at the Stadium some thirty years ago. I don't suppose anybody here knows it but Colonel Ruppert called my father after that incident and said, quite flatly, "I'll fire him if you say so, Bill."

My father would have none of it, of course, and told the Colonel that Barrow was all right, he'd just lost his head. He told much the same thing to his own managing editor who wanted to make a circulation *cause célèbre* of the affair and have Barrow arrested.

The managing editor never forgave my father for this. It does seem ironic that the only newspaperman who actively disliked my father was his boss. And he disliked him for trying to do somebody a favor.

My father did a far better job at forgiving Barrow than I could ever do—but then he did just about everything somewhat better than I could. In fairness to Barrow, when the opportunity came for him to repay my father's favor he did so. When Barrow permitted baseball broadcasting of Yankee games the Giants and Dodgers had to go along. This was a big feather in my father's cap because his employer, General Mills, wanted those broadcasts.

My father's kindness took many forms. When Ban Johnson was fired my father was in Chicago for the baseball meetings and somehow he had the story exclusively. He gave it to every writer at the meeting.

Inasmuch as I would never do such a thing, I asked him why he was so generous with such a magnificent beat. He said he had to walk through some tunnel or other back to his hotel in Chicago and as he walked he thought about his baseball-writing friends. The fact that they had all been laughing and drinking together just a few hours before on the train. There was no satisfaction to him in beating his own friends on any story. Particularly a great story, as the Johnson dismissal certainly was.

I remember one day in the Chase Hotel in St. Louis, back in 1936. He was covering the pennant-bound Giants; I was covering the cellar-bound Dodgers, directed by Casey Stengel, a nongenius then. There was one room in the Chase in those pre-air-conditioned days that was always cool. The nice lady who checked the teams in always gave that room

61

to my father. And, oddly, to me although I was only a 23-year-old busher.

The Dodgers checked in about an hour after the Giants left and there was a letter waiting for me on the bureau. It was from him and ran three long pages, in ink although he had a typewriter handy.

This is what it said, in a condensed version:

Dear Billy:

You are writing very well and I am so pleased when my friends tell me that. But I wish you would stop making fun of the ballplayers. It makes for amusing reading, good reading, but it hurts some nice people, many of whom you don't even know.

The fellows with the Dodgers are suffering more than you could realize. They are trying so hard to hang on in the only business they know. They are not very good, their days are numbered, and their wives and children read you. They read everybody writing about their husbands and fathers.

You shouldn't say that they are good because they are not. And, if a man loses a game you can do nothing but point out that he lost the game. But when you are cutting loose with one of those cynical lines of yours, think if it's really worth the pain it causes.

That's how he felt about honest men doing an honest job, no matter how poorly. On the other hand, I was covering a prizefight camp one time and I wrote: "Max Baer boxed twice today. Once for the movie cameras and once with live sparring partners. Maxie did much better against the cameras than the humans who could fight back."

A camp hanger-on, a fight manager, read my black copy and called Ed Frayne, my sports editor. And my father's. The hanger-on felt that perhaps Mr. Frayne wouldn't want to have Mr. Baer ridiculed. Mr. Frayne called for my dupe,

FRACTURED CONFAB

"Blonde...at 3 o'clock!!!!"

63

read it, and told the hanger-on to forget it. My father over-heard the conversation and got on the phone to me at once.

He didn't swear much, as you know, but he was irate. He told me about the phone call from the fight manager. Then he said, "Don't let that towel-swingin' sunavabitch tell you what to write."

He was a great man, gentleman. A great newspaperman, a great editor, and, my God, he was a great father.

Confessions of a Baseball Fan

BY JOHN K. HUTCHENS

It was a summer day in 1913, and the sun shone hot and bright on the old West Side baseball park in Chicago, then the home of the Cubs. I was eight years old, and I had been waiting a long time for this, the first major league game I would ever see.

Coming in on the train that Sunday afternoon from the suburb where we lived, my father had said: "Now don't ex-pect too much. The Cubs aren't much good this year." I knew the Cubs were no longer great—the wonderful Tinker-to-Evers-to-Chance machine had broken up a year or so be-fore—and I knew also that my father was making a joke. Any time the Cubs were playing the Giants you could expect a good deal. The fans sitting near us on the train had said so. The Giants, they had said, were a lot of——, in particu-lar their manager, John J. McGraw.

Now we were in the park, and there was McGraw him-self, squat and truculent, coaching at third base, jeering at my heroes on the field and at the crowd behind him. And the crowd was yelling back. It was reminding Fred Snodgrass,

Giant outfielder, of the muff that had cost the Giants the World Series with the Red Sox the preceding autumn and Fred Merkle of his failure to touch second base and the pennant that boner lost for the Giants in 1908. The afternoon wore on, golden and exciting. Dust and drama, speed and skill, big Jeff Tesreau's spitball cracking past confused Chicago batters until, finally, our Frank ("Wildfire") Schulte slid under Chief Meyers, the Giant catcher, with the winning run in the last inning while straw hats sailed onto the field, the crowd told Mr. McGraw what it thought of him and his —— —— ball club, and an eight-year-old in the grandstand sat back exhausted, limp with vicarious triumph.

So I became a baseball fan.

No baseball fan has to explain his mania to any other baseball fan. They are a fraternity. It is less easy, often it is hopeless, to try to explain it to anyone else. You grow technical, and you do not make sense. You grow sentimental, and you are deemed soft in the head. How, the benighted outsider asks you with no little condescension, can you grow sentimental about a cold-blooded professional sport?

But there it is, the sentiment, and I suspect it is a greater factor in baseball than in any other sport. My own youthful days in the Chicago ball parks were spent in the company, so to speak, of great men, the memory of whom has been as balm in more complicated times. Not all of them, I later discovered, were admirable characters, but on the ball field they were artists and to watch them was at once pleasurable and instructive.

One boy quickly learned, for example, though not aware at the time of the analogy, that the race is to the swift. He learned it by watching Tyrus Raymond Cobb go from first base to third on a bunt. He got an inkling of the nature of showmanship by seeing Hal Chase, the peerless first base-

66

man, make the easy chances look hard and the hopeless ones look easy. He grasped the essence of the professional performer—timing and economy—whenever Walter Johnson took the mound and with that easy, sidearm delivery fired his fast one past batters who were lucky to reach him for a foul.

Yes, I confess with no embarrassment whatever to a mental file of action pictures that can stir me even now: Tris Speaker streaking back from short center field to deep center to pull down the long drives; Honus Wagner, bowlegged and clumsy-seeming at the plate, lunging at the ball—and connecting with it, even in his old age; the consummate grace of Napoleon Lajoie, the second baseman, then also at the end of his career; Jimmy Archer, the catcher, throwing from a crouch and picking surprised runners off first base; Joe Jackson bringing his big black bat around in a grooved swing that was the perfection of hitting style; Cobb riding high into third base, spikes flashing in that terrific hook slide. . . . The list could go on for a long time, but you see what I mean.

However, there is more than nostalgia in this, else one would rest comfortably on his memories of other times, like an old grad boring the undergraduates at a twenty-fifth reunion. But a fan who is a fan keeps going to ball games, year in, year out.

The game is always there. It has continuity. Unlike football with its raucous flurry of autumn weekends, it not only is on view for five and a half months of the year but it lives through the winter in the Hot Stove league. No other sport is so conducive to long conversations replete with angles, figures, personalities and the stuff of argument in the home and at the soda fountain. From World Series to spring training, a long stretch by the calendar, is—for the fan—a brief while in which to pore over old score cards, peruse baseball's Bible, the *Sporting News,* and prepare himself for the next marathon.

Awaiting it, he knows that the game he sees in the spring will be familiar to him. That's another thing I like about it. The face of it will not have been altered through the winter by a lot of new rules. The general style of play has indeed changed over the years—and not altogether, I think, for the better. Personally, being of the old school, I favor the run-at-a-time strategy as opposed to the powerhouse production of runs needled by the lively ball. To me, the spectacle of Cobb stretching a double into a triple was always more exhilarating than a Ruthian homer.

But—and this is part of the game's continuity—any honest fan will admit that the giants have had worthy successors. A Babe Ruth fades; a Joe DiMaggio and a Ted Williams saunter up to the plate. A Johnson runs down; a Lefty Grove and, later, a Bob Feller step onto the mound. Newcomers do not crowd out the memory of old masters, but they at least carry on the great tradition. And, though it may be heresy to say so, some of them may be even better.

The tradition, in the case of my generation, especially in Chicago, was once put to a fearful test. That, of course, was the Black Sox scandal that broke a year after the 1919 World Series in which—incredibly—eight players on one of the greatest teams ever assembled sold out to the gamblers. You would have had to be one of us to know the downright agony of it. Any of us could have been the sobbing kid who reputedly stood outside the courthouse and cried out to the great Jackson, "Say it ain't so, Joe!" Throughout that winter of 1920-21 we muttered bitterly of the betrayal. But in the spring we came around. There were still Cobb, Sisler, Hornsby, Collins, Johnson—and the mighty pitcher transformed into an outfielder, George Herman Ruth. We sat

68

again in the sun behind third base. There were still heroes.

Some of my early fanaticism, I admit, has passed with the years. It was an off-day, in my baseball-smitten youth, when I could not recite the hitting, pitching and fielding averages of any given member of the White Sox and the Cubs, and fill in around the edges with such personal data as their superstitions, weights, heights and home towns, together with their minor league records before they came up from the bushes. There isn't time now for all that. Still, when I know that I am going to spend an afternoon at what sports writers used to call the ball orchard, I feel a touch of the old excitement. For two or three hours, under happy conditions, I will be watching a drama compounded of craft and power, enacted by people who for the most part know their trade.

As I say, it isn't quite so thrilling to me as in the old days, when every player on the home team was one of nature's noblemen and every fellow in a visitor's uniform a personal enemy. Not every game I see nowadays strikes me as being a nine-inning Trojan War, to be refought later in endless detail on the way home. But I would say, and the experts can make of this what they will, that I have never seen a ball game that I regretted having taken the trouble to go to.

For one of the good things about being a baseball fan is that you don't have to be an expert. (If I ever had any illusions about being one I got over them one afternoon when, sitting beside Red Barber in the broadcasting booth at Ebbets Field, I heard that greatest of baseball reporters discussing fine points I had missed entirely.) You have to know the fundamentals, of course, and you ought to have some background on individual players; but that is all that is really necessary. Unless you are a Dodger fan, or otherwise partisan by nature, you can sit there and relax.

69

Indeed, now that I no longer am either unduly elated or depressed by the result of a game, much of my pleasure in baseball comes from simply being in a ball park. It is a cheerful place; a fine-looking and a gay one, too, with the sun ablaze over green grass, flags fluttering in the breeze of a summer afternoon, the crack of bat on ball, the echoing of players and the droning hum of a big crowd. All around you are people who have come there to enjoy themselves.

Very important, this sociable air. A race track swarms with sweaty oafs intent on getting something for nothing and sullen if they fail. A fight crowd is exciting and excited, and vaguely pathologic. But a baseball crowd, excepting the stray cranks and exhibitionists, is a neighborly lot. Despite the shadow of 1919, it can be quite certain—as a race or a fight crowd cannot be—that what it is seeing is honestly performed. Its members get acquainted easily, trade observations casually, as becomes a land of free speech. They want to see the home team win, but they are generous to the opposition, even in Brooklyn. They make a lot of noise, they let off steam via the Bronx cheer and the boo, but they seldom mean it. Almost never does the ball park hear the fight crowd's bloodcry.

So, for an afternoon, I sit up in pleasant surroundings, including the sun, and enjoy myself and my associates in the fraternity of fandom. As the game goes on I not only like it for what it is but I get to thinking of other games and other players, and I like that, too. Bobby Doerr goes back of second to rob Charlie Keller of a single to center, and I remember other great keystone sackers I have seen, Eddie Collins and Gehringer and Hornsby, and so on around the diamond and through the day. I like the sudden, sharp yell of the crowd when a batter catches hold of one with the tying run at first, and the electric tension that goes through a park when a runner and an outfielder's throw are staging a race for the plate. I like the peanut butcher's yapping chant up and down the aisles. In short, I like being for a brief while in a good-natured place that is a self-sufficient little world of its own. This can probably be called escapism. All right, then, it is escapism.

If memory serves, seeing a ball game was not always so pastoral. In the stands, as on the field, things are more orderly than I seem to remember they were at that old West Side park in Chicago. And that is all right with me, now. I do not find Mr. Williams, of Boston, a villain when he busts one into the right-field stand. I find him a great ballplayer, and I suspect I enjoy the sight the more for the detachment with which I view it.

I suspect also, however, that no one ever recovers absolutely from the kind of early conditioning I had. Picking up the sports page in the morning, I can still feel something like a pang if the Cubs or the White Sox lost a ball game the day before. And if they both lost, I can even feel slightly depressed until about 10 A.M.

South America, Take It Away

BY BUCK CANEL

In the mid-1870's a scattering of Cuban boys started coming to the U.S.A. for their education and, among other things, learned to play a newfangled game called "beisbol" which they promptly took back to their Caribbean homeland. The "locos," as they were called by their insular friends who much preferred bullfighting and pelota to the crazy "gringo" game of the bat, the ball and "ridiculous short

71

pants," persisted in their endeavors and in a few years Cuba had a few beisbol clubs. At the turn of the century, under the impetus given the game by the Spanish-American War and the consequent "invasion" of Cuba by hordes of American soldiers, beisbol became Cuba's national game, so much so that by 1914 guys like Mike Gonzalez, Dolph Luque, Armando Marsans, Monolo Cueto, "Count" Almeida and others had already started the flow of Cuban major-leaguers that was destined to produce so many fine competitors.

The "contagion" from Cuba spread to other Caribbean areas. Puerto Rico started to play beisbol soon after and it was a Puerto Rican team that introduced the game to Venezuela early in the century. Meanwhile the game had "wet backed" its way across the Rio Grande into Mexico, the Central American countries and Panama.

Today beisbol is played in many Latin lands and it's even making inroads in countries like Peru, Colombia, Ecuador, and others where soccer is the king of sports. Roughly speaking, one can trace the world ascendancy of the U.S.A. and the decline of the British Empire by the corresponding graphs of soccer and baseball.

By 1905 professional leagues were in full swing in Cuba and Puerto Rico and the quality of play was so good that barnstorming American teams—notably the 1909 Detroit Tigers and the 1914 Philadelphia Athletics—were soundly drubbed in Havana. Gonzalez, Luque and the rest were only samples of the great players Cuba produced between the turn of the century and the lifting of the color line in 1947. Such Cuban Negro stars as José de la Caridad Mendez, Martin Dihigo, Alejandro Oms and many others would have been major-league stars in any era. John McGraw, who used to winter in Havana, once said he would have paid $100,000

72

for Mendez, a fireballing right-hander, if he could have whitewashed him.

Now, Cuban baseball under Fidel Castro's Communist regime is no more. The bearded dictator has abolished professional sport in the island and has advised Cubans they better stick to soccer and other Soviet games. Even though Castro himself was a fair-to-middling right-handed pitcher in his student days and was a red-hot fan even when he was "revoluting" up in the Sierra Maestra Mountains, baseball now savors too much of "Yanqui imperialismo."

Castro was so much of a baseball fan that when this writer interviewed him in January, 1959, in Cuba he indulged in the fan's ancient privilege of second-guessing a World Series manager. Telling me he had heard my broadcast of the 1958 series by shortwave up in his mountain retreat, he asked vehemently: "Tell me; why did Haney pitch Spahn in the sixth game? I would have pitched that 'hombre de la saliva, Lew Burdette.' "

Without Cuba, the Caribbean Baseball Federation has lost much of its zing, even though Puerto Rico, Venezuela, and the combined Panama-Nicaragua Winter Leagues are now preparing to play the Caribbean World Series in San Juan. Many of the Cuban major-leaguers are playing in the other Caribbean leagues. Mike de la Hoz, Leo Cardenas of Cincinnati, Orlando Peña, Octavio Rojas, Tony Gonzalez, Pancho Herrera, Leo Posada and many other Cuban stars are playing in Puerto Rico, Venezuela and Panama-Nicaragua, having decided not to return to Cuba while Castro is in power.

Others, such as Minnie Minoso, Camilo Pascual and Pedro Ramos, decided to stay in the States as they cannot play winter ball because of the rule that forbids big-leaguers

73

with more than three years' experience to participate in tourneys except in their countries of origin.

In the Dominican Republic, political tensions put a halt to the winter season. Joe Schultz, Don Hoak and Ken Silvestri were down in Santo Domingo as managers when the "troubles" came and besides such Dominican major-leaguers as the three Alou brothers, Juan Marichal, and "Speedy" Gonzalez, several American big-leaguers including Jim Donohue, Willie Davis, Hal Jones, Jim Schaeffer, Gino Cimoli and others were on the local rosters. They were confined to their hotels for weeks after having played only a few games, but no harm came to any of them. On the contrary, they were all paid off in full and the boredom they endured between dips in the pool of their luxury hotel was all they had to complain about.

The flow of Latin major-leaguers that started some fifty years ago is bound to continue, judging by the young talent I've seen in my jaunts through the Caribbean area. There are many fine young players coming up in Puerto Rico, Venezuela, Mexico, Panama, Nicaragua and the Dominican Republic. We'll see some of them soon in the major leagues, following in the footsteps of the Gonzalezes, Luques, Carrasquels, Minosos, Pascuals, Clementes, Avilas, Cepedas and Powers. A guess would be that, with Cuba out of the picture, Puerto Rico will send us the lion's share of Latin big-leaguers in the next few years. The tremendous inspiration given to Puerto Rican youngsters by the feats of Bob Clemente, Orlando Cepeda and Luis Arroyo during the 1961 season is sure to produce many an aspiring big-leaguer on sandlots from San Juan to Ponce, Mayagüez and Caguas.

A recent poll among the Latin big-leaguers which I made for France Presse News Agency, produced the following All-

FRACTURED SQUAWK

YER OUTA THE GAME!

'He said I — ruined his camera angle'

Star team of Latins who have performed at some time or other in the National or the American League:

Orlando Cepeda (Giants) 1b . . . . (Puerto Rico)
Bob Avila (Cleveland) 2b . . . . (Mexico)
Vic Power (Cleveland) 3b . . . . (Puerto Rico)
Chico Carrasquel (White Sox) ss . . . . (Venezuela)
Minnie Minoso (White Sox) lf . . . . (Cuba)
Luis Olmo (Dodgers) cf . . . . (Puerto Rico)
Bob Clemente (Pirates) rf . . . . (Puerto Rico)
Mike Guerra (Senators) c . . . . (Cuba)
Mike Gonzalez (Cardinals) c . . . . (Cuba)
Dolph Luque (Reds, Giants, Dodgers) p . . . . (Cuba)
Camilo Pascual (Twins) p . . . . (Cuba)
Pedro Ramos (Twins) p . . . . (Cuba)
Hiram Bithorn (Cubs) p . . . . (Puerto Rico)
Mike Fornieles (Red Sox) p . . . . (Cuba)
Alex Carrasquel (Senators) p . . . . (Venezuela)

On the bench would be such players as Luis Aparicio (Venezuela); Tony Gonzalez (Cuba); the Alou brothers (Dominican Republic); Sandy Amoros (Cuba); Chico Hernandez (Cuba); Bob Estalella (Cuba); Armando Marsans (Cuba); Nap Reyes (Cuba); and many others too numerous to mention.

So, in spite of Mr. Castro and his cries of "Yanqui, no," Latins are bound to give "beisbol" a resounding "sí" for many years to come.

Toots Shor and Friend

Since the mid-thirties, when he took over the old Tavern in New York, following the death of Billy Lahiff, Toots Shor has been the host most favored by big league ballplayers, professional football players, fighters, jockeys, train-

77

ers and race horse owners, golfers, college football coaches and sports writers. From all over the country they gather in what he calls his saloon to enjoy his company and, very often, to seek his counsel.

None ever was closer to him—nor is any closer to him now—than Joe DiMaggio. Joe is, by nature, a very shy man. When he first met Toots he was a real introvert.

Joe Gould and Jim Braddock first took him into the Tavern in 1936, when he was in his first season with the Yankees, and Braddock was heavyweight champion of the world. Braddock isn't much of a talker either, but compared to DiMaggio he was eloquent that night. As they were breaking up, Toots asked the champion's manager:

"Can the boy talk?"

"Yes," Gould said, "but I guess he don't like to."

Telling the story, some time later, Toots said:

"We got along great together right from the start, but he didn't talk much, even to me, especially when there was anybody else around. One night, when he and Lefty Gomez and I were having dinner and Lefty, as usual, was making everybody who came up to the table laugh, and even gabbing with people at other tables, Joe said to me, kind of sad like:

" 'I wish I could be like Lefty but I can't and I know people who meet me go away saying to themselves that I am a swell-headed Dago.'

"Of course they didn't say anything of the kind—or if some of them did, they were ignorant creeps—and who needs them?

"Joe paid me one of the greatest compliments I ever had. He and Tom Meany were doing a magazine piece and Tom called me one afternoon and said:

" 'I am with your friend, DiMag. I just asked him how he would make a play . . .'

"As I recall it," Toots said, "it was a cutoff. Anyway, Tom said:

" 'He told me how he would make it and I told him the way I had learned it from Uncle Robbie and John McGraw and he said I should call you and ask you how you would make it.

"Can you imagine that? He wouldn't go along with Uncle Robbie or McGraw. He left the decision up to *me*!

"Everybody in baseball had the greatest respect and, I might say, affection for DiMag. With all the ability he had, they still wanted to help him when, as it happens to all of us, he needed help. One night when Jimmy Dykes was managing the White Sox, he was in the joint for dinner. This was just after the third game of a four-game series and Joe hadn't got a hit yet and Jimmy said to me:

" 'When you see the Dago again, tell him I said he should loosen up. He's lunging at the ball.'

"I called Joe that night and told him what Dykes had said. The next day—boy, did he hit the Sox pitchers! A home run . . . a double . . . two singles! He ruined them!

"That night, on his way to the train, Dykes called me.

" 'You —— ——!' he said. 'At least you could have waited for me to get out of town!'

"DiMag, as you remember, had a tough time in the 1949 World Series with the Dodgers. He was a walking pneumonia case when the series opened but he insisted on playing, although he was getting weaker all the time, and with the last game coming up he had made only one hit. The night before that game Hank Greenberg was in and he said to me:

" 'Tell Joe to use a lighter bat tomorrow.'

"It was late . . . too late to call Joe . . . so I went out to Ebbets Field early the next day and told him what Hank

79

had said. So he got a lighter bat and made his second hit of the series—a home run.

"Joe has helped a lot of fellows, too. Charley Keller and Tommy Henrich were great favorites of his and when they were having trouble he worried about them more than he did about himself, even though he might be going just as lousy, if not more so, at the same time. One night he called me up and said:

" 'I'm at the hotel and I got Charley with me. Come on over.'

" 'Why don't you come over here?' I asked him.

"And he said: 'You know Charley. He's bashful, anyway, and right now he's down and don't want to meet people. I thought if you could come over here, we could sit around with him and maybe cheer him up.'

" 'What's the matter with him?' I asked.

" 'He's hitting two-thirty,' Joe said.

" 'And what are you hitting?'

"And he said, 'Two-fifty.'

" 'You're a fine one to be cheering him up,' I said. 'I'll be right over before you cry yourselves to sleep.' "

F. G.

Fun Can Be Baseball
And Twice as Versa

BY ARTHUR ("BUGS") BAER

A fellow who figured baseball was fun couldn't have done better than to have started with Clark Griffith's Senators in 1912. Griff and I hit Washington from different directions after McAleer had rung up five No Sales in five tries. Since 1901 the Washingtons had been in the cellar so often they were growing mushrooms in right field. They had never finished better than sixth in eleven seasons. Which saved the management money for nobody ever asked a Washington player for an autographed baseball.

In 1912 Griff inherited more clowns than Barnum's widow. Outside of Walter Johnson he had a sore-armed pitching staff that could have warmed up inside a greenhouse. Griff took this outfit from last place to contention. Griff won sixteen straight with this outfit without one cheer from the home rooters. Fifteen were won on the road. The sixteenth was a home game but only United States senators, congressmen, generals, admirals, high bureaucrats and diplomats got in. There was a small bleacher for loyal fans but Griff raised the price of tickets double. The Washingtons dropped their seventeenth game in Philadelphia. Loyal Washington fans went to that town to root against Griff. The boost was the fault of the Washington directors who had a free list longer than the Weather Bureau.

The only players the fans didn't hoot were the Big Train (Walter Johnson) and Zeb Milan. Johnson was Griff's ace in the hole. The trouble was the rest of the deck was in the hole with him. One of the pitchers, Dixie Walker, sat on the bench so long he ran sitting down. He was the father of the Walker boys who were good outfielders and batters. Long Tom Hughes was another pitcher who eased up a hard-bottomed season on the bench by wearing his sliding pads under his fanny.

Joe Engel was a husky kid from Mt. St. Mary's in Maryland. His father ran a saloon on E Street between the *Times* and the *Post*. Newspapermen from both papers were willing to split the difference. Papa Engel never got tired of setting up beers while he spoke pridefully of "My poy Choe." And that's what Choe was called from then out. He had swift curves, but less control than a boy with a busted kite string. When My Poy Choe lost a morning game in Boston, one to nothing, he got a hundred messages of congratulation. His Washington pals figured that was the closest My Poy Choe would ever come to winning a game. And they were as right as the answers in the back of the book. The afternoon game was pitched by Walter Johnson and was the start of the sixteen-game winning streak which statisticked that one in Boston, four in St. Louis, four in Chicago, four in Detroit, three in Cleveland and none for the little boy who lives down the lane. They didn't win a game in Philadelphia. The records show that when Johnson wasn't pitching he was pitching for the others in relief. Engel's name appears once in the string but he was jacked for Carl Cashion and Mullin. Twice Griff used five pitchers to win on successive days in Chicago. Twice he used four pitchers to win in Detroit and Cleveland and six times Griff required three throwers to get the bacon crisp. Winning sixteen straight needed forty-nine pitchers. Time and tide wait for no man but this mob sure loaded a ferry-boat.

Griff had the decency to deny he ever traded a pitcher for a bird dog. He could have used a retriever trained to pick up bunion pads, mustard plasters and ankle braces. The pitcher's name was Fowler and the reason the bird dog's name didn't appear in the line-up was because it was a training camp transaction. The party of the second part was Joe Cantillon who managed Washington in 1907, 1908 and 1909. He tried to trade the Big Train to Minneapolis in 1909. That was the year Johnson proved he could throw a lamb chop past a wolf. The arm is quicker than the blink.

82

The reason for the trade? Before the 1909 season was dry behind its deficit Cantillon was managing Minneapolis. He was guaranteeing himself job insurance. With fringe benefits.

Griff tried his hand at pitching his first season in Washington but he couldn't throw a meat ball past a fat boy.

In addition to the Big Train he had Cashion, Groom, Boehling, Altrock, Walker, Gallia and Doc Ayres. Doc was kissing cousin to the Allen Gang that shot up the Blue Ridge courthouse when Uncle Allen was being tried for ambushing a McCoy. The West Virginia code of nonpartisan skirmishing called for a five-yard start. Uncle Allen gave the McCoy a five-yard start but it was uphill. Altrock took the Clown title away from Germany Schaefer by riding a painted fraternity mule backward into training camp. But nobody on the team was funny enough to make the owners laugh. First-string catcher was Gabby Street who caught a ball dropped from the top of Washington Monument. But he dropped everything the Big Train threw from sea level. He quit in 1909 when his catching hand swelled up so that he looked like a violinist on his way to work.

There was a quiver on the Wall Street seismograph when the Washington directors paid ten grand for Chick Gandil a first-sacker from Montreal. Chico had been a heavyweight fighter along the Mexican border. Later reports from the Reds-White Sox 1919 World Series indicated a ninety-foot ring was too big for him. At second was Ray Morgan hungover from last season. Also hung-over from last night. He was Peck's Bad Boy and fielded grounders like his legs were wickets in a croquet game. Griff got fed up with Morgan's Midnight Raids and sent way out west for a California wonder named Joe Gedeon. He was ticketed through Charlottesville on a through-train but refused to get off a Pullman

83

sleeper in a midnight blizzard. Germany Schaefer ran along the frost-bitten platform yelling, "Gideon, Gideon." That got us a big fat nothing for the engineer thought we were hollering "Giddap, Giddap." As the wheels started to grind northward a red head popped out of a jack-in-the-box window and grunted, "Whattchawant?" "You," shouted Germany who became Dutch Schaefer along about the time that sauerkraut was re-named Liberty cabbage and frankfurters became hot dogs. "I ain't getting off in a blizzard for nobody," yelled Gedeon who was seeing snow for the first time in his sun-kissed career. He rode the Pullman into Washington and came back a week later. Griff's idea of the sunny south was any ticket that didn't cost over seven dollars. Ordinarily he would have sent Gedeon packing without even a trial meal at the training table. But he was shorter-handed than a monkey in a switch-tower and Gedeon lasted a couple of months. He hit .400 until June and then he folded up like a dude's handkerchief. He proved this later with the Yanks and then went back to Hollywood where the snow is either talcum powder or corn flakes.

George McBride was a fixture at shortstop. There was no better description of this middle-aged gentleman who strayed neither to the right nor to the left. George was as stiff-legged as a stuffed crane. And used his bat more as a protection than as a weapon of offense.

There was a little fellow at third named Eddie Foster who admired Billy Sunday and eventually became an evangelist. It was Eddie who took me from cartooning to reporting. When the slashing Ty Cobb cut little Eddie from ankle to knee I drew a cartoon depicting Cobb stopping at a barbershop to have his spikes honed. The next day I got a twenty-page letter on Hotel Willard paper starting "You snake in the grass" and gathering vilification with every line. Cobb mentioned

84

this in his biography. I took the letter to our sporting editor, Louie Dougher, but Louie outsmarted me. He didn't print it. Or I would have been in New York five years sooner.

In addition to Germany Schaefer, the man who stole first base, Griff had in center a man who stole seventy bases a season and never got mentioned. Ty Cobb was stealing eighty and ninety. Today thirty will get you in the Hall of Fame and a player is considered a terrific runner if he doesn't get thrown out at first on a base on balls.

Milan finally stole eighty-eight bases in 1912 and was awarded second prize. First prize was a box of wet matches.

In right field most of the season was Danny Moeller an athlete who was in and out of the hospital like a florist's delivery boy. Danny covered a lot of ground, could field and run. But every time he threw a ball his shoulder became disarticulated. Danny would grunt in mounting waves of pain unable to move. You know what that meant to runners like Cobb, Speaker and other scooters. Trainer Mike Martin would manipulate the errant pump-handle into traction and wrap Danny in more adhesive tape than Pharaoh's uncle Ptot-Ptot. Mike tried slings, corsets and bandages but bingo! out popped the humerus from the clavicle. . . .

Griff replaced Moeller with his first two Cubans, Calvo and Acosta, and that was when the Spanish flew. They disputed every decision in a strange language that certainly should have earned fines and suspensions. These two all-Havana foolers could run, catch and throw. But they reversed Gabby Street's catch from the top of the monument. At bat the Cubanolas hit nothing but straight-up pops that a man in the window of Washington Monument could catch.

Whatta you know? In his first year Griff manipulated this squad of culls into second place. And he was working for a bunch of stockholders who had all their grandchildren thinking milk was blue.

I was a clown, too, and I hit Washington when the berries were ripe. I learned from Griff and I learned from Mike Flynn of Munsey's *Times* when I wired back a classical description of a Charlottesville blizzard. Mike telegraphed me, "Stick to baseball. We get our weather reports from the government."

Griff had some players like Herring, Schegg, Kenworthy, Morley and others, but they were normal and went at the waiver price. The ones I think of oftenest after fifty years are the manager who tried to feather-bed his switch to Minneapolis by stuffing the mattress with the Big Train, greatest of pitchers; Tyrus Cobb who didn't stop at the barbershop to have his spikes honed and the benched Discobolus who ran sitting down; the man who stole first and the brash rook who wouldn't detrain on his very first trip to the majors.

It takes all kinds of people to make a world and Griff was their manager.

I *Remember*

BY SENATOR FORD

The New York Giants were playing the Chicago Cubs on September 23, 1908, at the Polo Grounds, with Christy Mathewson pitted against Giant Killer Jake Pfeister. In the last of the ninth the score was tied, 1–1. There were two out. Moose McCormick was on third, and Fred Merkle— playing his first full game with the Giants—was on first. Shortstop Al Bridwell, the Giants' great clutch hitter, rifled a line drive into center for a clean hit. Merkle ran part way to second, saw McCormick cross the plate with the winning run, and promptly high-tailed it to the clubhouse to duck the crowd that was swarming out on the field.

Eagle-eye Johnny Evers, the Cub second baseman, seeing that Merkle hadn't touched second, yelled to center fielder Solly Hoffman to throw him the ball. Hoffman's throw was on the sour side, and the ball landed in the merry throng that was milling around near the Cub dugout.

Now, here's where a little-known bit of drama took place. In those days, baseball clubhouses weren't equipped with strong boxes to safeguard the players' valuables while they were on the field. It was the custom to appoint one of the players—usually a pitcher who wasn't scheduled to work that day—to play watchdog to the players' jewelry and money. On this occasion, the job was assigned to a young Cub pitcher named Floyd Kroh. All during the game our hero sat on the bench clutching the little black satchel containing the Cubs' treasure. But when Hoffman's bad throw

87

landed near the Chicago dugout, a spectator picked it up and put it in his pocket.

With Evers yelling and screaming for the ball, something stirred within Kroh's youthful breast. He suddenly sensed that there was dirty work brewing at the crossroads—the crossroads, in this case, being second base. So Floyd dashed out, still holding the bag, and asked the fan for the ball. The culprit refused. Kroh then decided to get it the hard way; he wrestled the guy for it. And he won. He got the ball and threw it to the Whirling Dervish at second base. Evers promptly touched the bag and claimed a force-out, and umpire Hank O'Day called Merkle out. It took him until the next day to do it, so the game was ruled a tie and had to be played over.

Now, here's where Old Man Retribution reared his ugly kisser. In order to grapple with the ball-grabbing fan, Kroh put the satchel down on the ground. After he had thrown the ball to Evers, he turned to retrieve the boodlebag, and found to his dismay that said satchel had vanished like cream in a cat's saucer. Some rude fan had picked it up and lit out with approximately $5,200 worth of Cub money and jewelry.

Most of the shenanigans pertaining to this play never did make sense to me. Why was Kroh allowed to be involved in a force play when he wasn't even in the game? And if he had any rights in the matter, why didn't he get an assist in the box-score? The odds are a million to one that these $64,000 questions will never be answered.

Now we come to some by-products of the Merkle case. In late September of 1908, the race was closer than two lovers on a sofa. The Giants, Pirates and Cubs thought they all had squatters' rights to first place.

Pittsburgh was in Chicago playing the last game of their

final series of the year when a few more weird incidents occurred. If the Pirates won this game, they would clinch the pennant. Both the Giants and the Cubs would be also-rans, and Merkle's alleged "boner" would be meaningless.

According to a comparatively recent account of this game by a baseball writer, the Cubs were leading, 2–0, in the ninth. But the Pirates filled the bases, and the tension mounted when second baseman Ed Abbaticchio sent a screamer down the left-field line into the seats. Umpire Hank O'Day hesitated momentarily, then boomed, "Foul ball!" The Cubs got Abbaticchio out and went on to win the pennant by beating the Giants in the playoff. This turned out to be another assist for O'Day, for it was later proved that old Hank was as wrong as a two-foot yardstick.

A few months later—too late to be of any help to Pittsburgh and Merkle—a female fan sued the Pittsburgh Club, claiming that she had been hit by Abbaticchio's drive and seriously injured. She had sworn statements from witnesses, and a ticket stub to show that she was sitting where the ball had landed. A check of the ball park's seating chart showed that she had been sitting in *fair* territory. Abbaticchio's hit hadn't been foul; actually it was a genuine grand-slam home run.

Being a stickler, I dug up the official court record of the trial, and although the two versions differed in detail, they did agree on one thing: Hank O'Day was wrong. Here is the story according to the record of the trial:

The ball wasn't hit to left field; it was hit to right field. And it didn't land in the seats at all. It came down into the overflow crowd that rimmed the field. And O'Day called it foul. As in the story version, the lady fan sued, but she lost the case. Why? Because it was proved at the trial that she was hit by Abbaticchio's drive while standing in fair ground, where she had no right to be. If she had been standing in foul territory, she might have won the case by arguing that the ball club was supposed to protect her.

And there you have a couple of stories to prove that in ten days Hank O'Day personally decisioned two ball clubs down the laundry chute.

Getting back to Merkle, it was a shame to make him the villain in the melodrama. How about a couple of demerits for his teammates? Just how fast asleep was the first-base coach? McGraw never blamed Merkle for the loss of the 1908 pennant. As a matter of fact, he raised Fred's salary the following year. Don't forget that the Giants dropped a Sunday double-header to the doormat Cardinals when all they had to do was to win one of these two games. And how about the three they lost in the final week of the season to a guy by the name of Harry Coveleski of the Phillies? If they had won just one of the games they blew in the last 17, Merkle would have been off the hook.

Merkle was a good, smart ballplayer, and he took the rap for doing what he had seen older ballplayers do all season. He was simply caught in a technicality. The great old umpire Bill Klem said, "It was the worst decision ever made in baseball."

Merkle once said, "I suppose when I die my epitaph will be, 'HERE LIES BONEHEAD MERKLE.'"

Heinie Zimmerman also had a famous boner tacked on him when Zim was as innocent as a Zim could be. This singular "skull" occurred in the fourth inning of the sixth game of the 1917 World Series between the Chicago White Sox and the New York Giants. The score, at the time, was 0–0. The build-up to the big scene was like this:

Eddie Collins opened the inning with a bouncer to Zimmerman, at third, and reached second when Heinie made a bad throw to Walter Holke at first. Shoeless Joe Jackson lifted a can of corn to short right field where Davey Robertson clumsily dropped it. Jackson, naturally, was safe at first, and Collins legged it to third. The next batter, Happy Felsch, dribbled one back to Rube Benton, the pitcher. The Rube, seeing that Collins was too far off third to get back, threw to Zimmerman. Instead of diving back to third, Collins did some agile jockeying and then suddenly streaked for the plate. Zimmerman lit out after him like a sex-starved beagle. There was nothing for Zim to do but hope that Collins would break a leg on the way in. That was the only chance Heinie had of catching him.

You may ask why Zimmerman didn't throw the ball to the catcher. That's a good question. The answer is that there was no catcher to throw it to. Catcher Bill Rariden had run over to back up the play at third, and was about 20 feet off the line. As a matter of fact, there wasn't anybody for Zim to throw the ball to except umpire Klem. And I doubt that old Bill would have caught it.

Obviously nobody, including the writers, actually knew what happened, and they all allowed Zimmerman to be awarded the goat's horns.

I met Art Fletcher, the Giants' shortstop, that night, and he cleared up the situation. The blame had been placed by manager McGraw on first baseman Holke for failing to cover the plate. And there you have the story of another question-mark "boner." Incidentally, the Giants lost the game, 4–2.

Whenever baseball fans get together for a hot-stove league session, the hilarious episode of the three Dodgers on third is bound to crop up.

It happened in the first game of a double-header with Boston on August 15, 1926, at Ebbets Field. It was a sizzling Sunday, and there was some added sizzling at third base in the seventh inning. In fact it reached the broiling point, and there were a few sets of well-grilled ears on the premises before it was over.

The Dodgers had scored a run and had loaded the bases to set the stage for Babe Herman's glorious gallop into history. Hank DeBerry was on third, Dazzy Vance on second and Chick Fewster on first, when the mighty Herman stepped up to the plate. The Babe caught a hard one on the end of his bat and sent a sky-high fly into faraway right center field. Then, with his head down and his hopes high, he lit out like Man o' War.

DeBerry could score from third whether the ball was caught or not, and he did. But Vance, who was unaccustomed to life on the base paths, thought the ball might be caught, and hovered timidly in the vicinity of second base. The ball hit the fence and began bouncing around in right field and Vance got to third and stopped. Evidently, being so far from home on the bases befuddled him. With Herman bearing down on him with careless abandon, poor Fewster had only one way to go. So he went on to third, with Herman right behind him. When he arrived at third, he was flabbergasted to find Vance backing and filling on the third-base line. It began to look like a Mack Sennett setup.

Herman wouldn't stop, Fewster couldn't and Vance didn't. He retreated to third, and Herman slid in ferociously. Fewster was sandwiched between them. Only the natural upholstery of the Messrs. Vance and Herman saved poor Fewster from looking like a bookmark. Meanwhile, outfielder Welsh had relayed the ball to second baseman Doc Gautreau, who in turn had thrown it to Oscar Siemer, the catcher, just as Vance, Fewster and Herman arrived simultaneously at third base. Catcher Siemer was no fool. He realized that he had no use for the ball because Old Home Week was being celebrated at third base, so he threw it to third baseman Ed Taylor. Now Taylor went into action. He began touching everybody in sight but umpire Ernie Quigley.

When Taylor looked at the umpire for a decision, Quigley remained as immovable as a marble statue, so Taylor touched them all in reverse order, and again looked at Quigley. Still no soap.

Suddenly, something rumbled in Gautreau's cerebellum. He saw a great light. So he snatched the ball from Taylor and started walking toward second base. He remembered that according to a baseball rule, a base runner who passes a preceding base runner is a naughty boy and should be called out.

With Herman already out for passing Fewster, Taylor could have touched Vance all afternoon without getting anywhere so long as Vance stayed anchored to the bag. So Gautreau decided that Fewster was the only vulnerable Dodger on the field. As little Doc approached Fewster, Chick scented a deep-purple plot and he began moving away. But as Gautreau came closer, Fewster picked up speed and lit out for the safety of the wide-open spaces of the outfield. Doc chased Chick, finally caught him, and touched him with the ball. But, alas, all this was wasted energy because Fewster had long since been called out for running three feet out of the base line to duck a fielder intent upon tagging him.

And there you have the story of how the illustrious Babe Herman doubled into a double play.

But for you Brooklyn fans there is balm in Gilead—or, in this case, balm in Gowanus. Did you ever hear how the unparalleled Yankees pulled a parallel back in the thirties that was worse than the Brooklyn gang-up? You didn't? Well, pull up a couch and get a load of this.

In a game between the Yankees and the Washington Senators, the score was 6–4 in the last half of the ninth, with one out. Lou Gehrig was on second, Dixie Walker was on first, and Tony Lazzeri was at bat. Tony whacked a screamer over Goose Goslin's noggin in right center that looked like it would at least tie the score. Gehrig, thinking the ball was catchable, stuck close to second. Walker, seeing it was uncatchable, took off from first like a big bird. When Gehrig saw what was happening, he got up a full head of steam and plodded toward third. As Lou rounded the far corner, Walker was practically playing "Me and My Shadow" with him, but both of them hesitated as Goslin's relay came in. By this time Lazzeri was past second and racing for third. The Yankee paragons now realized that an overcrowded situation was developing around third base, and that they were about to borrow a leaf from the Dodgers' book. So Gehrig and Walker pulled up stakes and headed for home, with Walker again so close to Gehrig that it looked like he was riding him piggy-back. But at the plate, like Leonidas at Thermopylae, stood Washington catcher Luke Sewell with a nice, shiny baseball in his hand. As the Yankee tandem arrived, he klunked them both with the ball for a double play. Tony Lazzeri had tripled into a double play!

One of the bona-fide boners that will forever occupy a nut niche in the Baseball Hall of Infamy was John Anderson's steal of second base with a man already on. This bit of futile larceny was committed in 1904 at the old Hilltop Grounds, where the Highlanders played their glorified rounders. Clark Griffith was managing the Hilltoppers at the time, and he always got a laugh out of the recollection of Anderson trying to steal second with the bases full.

Heinie Mueller, of the St. Louis Cardinals, might be classed as a carbon copy—a ninth carbon copy—of Hamlet. Like Shakespeare's melancholy Dane, it was difficult to figure out whether Heinie was a deep thinker or just crazy.

One day the Cards were playing the Cubs, and manager Branch Rickey briefed center fielder Mueller thusly: "Son, when you see that our pitcher has been signaled to throw a slow ball, move in 20 feet. Go back to the fence when a fast ball is called for."

Mueller carried out Rickey's orders, moving in on slow pitches and out on the fast ones. The baseballwise bleacherites of Sportsman's Park soon got hep to what was going on. "Slow ball!" they'd chant as Mueller moved in, and "Fast ball!" as Heinie moved out. Like the Chinese water torture, this soon got on Mueller's nerves. Finally, with the bases full, a fast ball was called for. To Rickey's utter dismay, Heinie advanced instead of retreating. The result was that the batter drove the ball over Mueller's head and broke up the game.

Branch remained calm—as is his wont. "Son," he said in a dulcet tone, "what went wrong? Didn't you get the fast-ball sign?"

"Sure I did," replied the pixie. "I got the sign all right. But I just thought I'd cross up those wise-guys in the bleachers."

It was the same irrepressible Mueller who, with a man on first, whacked a ball over the fence and then got himself called out for running hell-bent past his own base runner.

Glenn Gardner was an innocent accomplice to Eddie Dyer's most embarrassing moment. This was in 1939 and Dyer was managing Houston of the Texas League. The

95

Buffs went into the ninth inning trailing 0–1. Gardner had pitched a whale of a game, and after he had shut out the other side in the last inning, Dyer consoled him. "Tough luck, kid," soothed Eddie. "You pitched a good game. It wasn't your fault. Go on and get your shower. I'll use a pinch hitter for you in our half of the ninth."

Gardner was scheduled to bat third. Jack Angle came up first and belted one nine miles over the left-field fence, tying the score. Now it was a new game. Dyer needed Gardner to finish if it went extra innings. Eddie looked around to tell Glenn to hit for himself. No Gardner.

"Where's Gardner?" he snapped nervously.

"Why, Skip, you told him to go to the clubhouse," the bat boy informed him in a tone of surprise. "He went."

"Go get him," Dyer said. "I want him to hit."

The bat boy took off.

"Where's your batter?" cried Rollie Naylor, the umpire. "Get a hitter up here!"

The bat boy came back and said Gardner was in the shower, but that he was coming as quickly as he could. Umpire Naylor was growing impatient.

"Now, Rollie," Dyer said, "my hitter had to go to the can, but he'll be right here."

"If he isn't," Rollie growled, "I'm gonna forfeit the game!"

"Look, Rollie," Dyer said, "my hitter is naked. You don't want him to come up here and bat in the nude, do you?"

"Naked!" sputtered Naylor, wide-eyed and growing red around the gills.

Finally, Gardner came running across the field, pulling on his shirt. He batted, made out, and couldn't pitch worth a lick for the rest of the game because he'd cooled off from the shower.

96

"We lost because I sent a pitcher I needed so badly to the showers," Dyer said.

I once asked Dizzy Dean if he had ever committed any boners. He said, "Yeah, one."

"What was it?"

"The day I signed with St. Louis," the Great One replied. "It was a boner because Sam Breadon and Branch Rickey never paid me what I was worth."

I told him I wasn't referring to that type of boner. What I meant was, had he pulled any real good ones on the ball field.

The Lucas, Arkansas, shrinking violet admitted that he had—once.

"The only skull I ever pulled on the field was in Cincinnati the last week of 1934. We were behind the Giants by two games, and we needed this one bad. So, naturally, I was pitchin'. When a guy has already won 26 ball games, a manager ain't gonna let no other bum pitch if he wants to win.

"Me and the Cards is leadin' 2–1, goin' into the bottom of the ninth. They had runners on second and third with two out. Lonnie Frey, a pretty fair country hitter—when he wasn't battin' against me—is up. My curve is good an' sharp, like nearly always, an' I run the count to two strikes an' no balls. Spud Davis is catchin' me, an' he signs me to fog my fast one through. Lonnie takes his cut and poops it up right over the mound.

" 'I got it!' I yells, wavin' Davis an' Rip Collins away.

"Get out o' there, Diz!" Davis yapped at me. "Let Rip take it!"

" 'It's mine,' I holler, waitin' for the ball to come down. But by now I'm thinkin' that maybe I better let Collins take it. He's a first baseman and he's supposed to take them pop-ups. My contract calls for me to pitch, and not to be bothered by no measly pop flies. And besides, I never was no great shakes at ketchin' pop-ups. It was probably my only weakness.

"Then Collins has to get real bighearted. He thinks maybe it'd be real nice to let ol' Diz ketch it an' win his own game. Well, you can guess what happens. Nobody ketches it. The ball flops between us for a hit, an' the Reds beat us, 3–2."

For once the great Dean's face was red, and it wasn't from sunburn.

The records attest that Goose Goslin rarely hit into a double play, yet his saddest day in baseball shows he hit into five of them in one game.

"I played the sun field all my life and made many a mistake," Goose said, "but my prize boner was attempting to apologize to Bill Klem—in a crowded elevator. We thought Klem had blown a couple that went against us at first base in the second game of the '34 World Series against the Cardinals. You now how it is. A ballplayer never thinks he's out. So we gave it to Klem. Every school kid knew how Bill hated to be called Catfish. Passing him between innings, Gerry Walker, myself and a few others called him Catfish and everything else that came to mind. We kept our heads down and just made the cracks as we went by.

"Paul Dean beat the Tigers that afternoon, which didn't help, and that night we left for Detroit.

"I happened to be staying at the same hotel where the Cardinals were parked. Klem was booked in there, too. The next morning it just so happened that I boarded the same elevator with him. It was jammed. But when I saw him, I extended my hand.

" 'Mr. Klem,' I said, 'I'm sorry about what happened yesterday.'

"Those were the last words I spoke, and I was a gabby

98

guy at the time. Klem called me every name that is not in the dictionary, and some more I'd never heard before. He said I was a jerk who wasn't fit to be in the major leagues. I didn't want to be thrown out of the World Series, so I turned my head away and tried to look nonchalant. He went right on bawling me out but I kept my mouth shut.

"My floor was one or two above Klem's, and when the elevator stopped to let him out at his landing, he put his foot in the door so the boy couldn't close it and kept blasting away. He really told me off.

"No fewer than 20 fans who were in the elevator wrote, telegraphed or told Commissioner Landis about what had happened. The judge called us both in after the World Series. Klem was fined $200 for vulgar and abusive language. I went scot free. I didn't ever hold it against Bill, and it further stressed a lesson I learned years before:

"Never talk back to an umpire.

"And never try to apologize—in a crowded elevator."

Gus Mancuso, recalling his biggest boner, says he'll never forget the 1937 World Series. Gus caught for the Giants against the Yankees in that one.

"Carl Hubbell and Lefty Gomez were hooked up in a real pitchers' battle up to the sixth inning of the first game," Gus remembers. "We were ahead, 1–0, going into the sixth. Then it started. Hubbell walked Gomez. We should have known what was coming. Why walk a guy who couldn't hit you with a bull fiddle? The only bat Gomez ever broke was one his kid left in the driveway; Lefty backed his car over it. A minute later we had Gomez picked off first base, but Burgess Whitehead dropped the ball. Frankie Crosetti singled Gomez to second. I called for another pitchout and threw down to Dick Bartell to catch Gomez off base, but Bartell dropped the ball. Red Rolfe hit a pop single to fill the bases, and then Joe DiMaggio singled home Gomez and Crosetti. We walked Lou Gehrig. Rolfe scored on Bill Dickey's single off Whitehead's glove. Myril Hoag hit to the infield, and DiMaggio was out at the plate. George Selkirk drove Gehrig and Dickey across with a single, and Bill Terry had me call time for a change of pitchers. Instead of coming out and telling me who the pitcher was going to be, Terry yelled at me from the bench. I thought Terry was yelling 'Gumbert,' so I told the umpire the new pitcher was Harry Gumbert. The umpire told the announcer and he told the crowd over the loudspeaker, 'Gumbert now pitching for the Giants.'

"Just as the announcement was made, Dick Coffman, who had been our bullpen pitcher all year, climbed over that little fence in left center field. By that time, Terry was waving his hands and hollering. So was everybody else in the park. When Coffman started to warm up, the Yankees put up a howl.

" 'Gumbert has been announced and you got to pitch him,' they protested. I knew then, but only then, that Terry had been yelling Coffman, not Gumbert.

"Harry Gumbert was sitting in a corner of the dugout. He hadn't even taken a warm-up pitch. The umpires ruled that he would have to dispose of one batter. Harry threw five warm-up pitches and a couple more to first base like he was trying to catch the runner, Selkirk. Tony Lazzeri finally hit a perfect double-play ball to Whitehead. That would have got us out of the inning and taken the curse off me, but Whitehead booted the ball. Hoag scored and Selkirk moved to third. Coffman came in and walked Gomez. That was probably a world's record—two bases on balls to Gomez in one inning. In all, the Yankees scored seven runs before we chased them out of there."

100

Benny Bengough, another catcher, says he has never forgotten the boner he pulled in 1925 before a packed house at Yankee Stadium. It was his first season as chief catcher for New York. "There's no sense in doing those things halfway," he said. "I was on first base. Our pitcher sacrificed me to second. While the Cleveland third baseman covered the bunt, Joe Sewell, the shortstop, moved to cover third base. Chick Fewster, the second baseman, had gone over to back up the first baseman in case of an overthrow on the bunt play. Edging to the shortstop's side of second base, I counted the Cleveland infielders. One, two, three, four. Yes, they were all present and accounted for. I took a bigger lead off second, meanwhile kidding the first baseman, George Burns, who had the ball.

" 'Why don't you throw it?' I shouted, lengthening my lead. So Burns threw it. Right to second base. Oh, boy, what a dope, throwing to second when there wasn't an infielder near it. I knew that I had 'em all accounted for. I spun around, and there, staring me in the face, was Tris Speaker, who had sneaked in from center field.

" 'Hi, Ben,' Tris grinned. 'See what I have here?' I was a dead duck on a rundown. Talk about boners, I'd have jumped into a gopher hole if there'd been one handy."

The successful hidden-ball trick is always humiliating to the victim. This goes double in spades when the sleeping beauty is warned ahead of time of what's up. This is just what happened to Gerald Walker when the Yankees pulled the stunt on him. But it's Walker's story, so we'll let him tell it.

"I was on second, and Red Ruffing and Frankie Crosetti told me that they were going to pull the trick on me. They kept telling me how dangerous it was not to stay alert on the

101

bases. I got sore and told them to mind their own business, and I didn't use parlor language. When I finished, I was shocked to find myself off second with Crosetti standing between me and the bag.

" 'Look what I've got, Gerry,' Frankie said, showing me a nice white baseball.

" 'Listen, you sonofabitch,' I told him, 'if you put that ball on me, I'll break your neck.' So Crosetti threw the ball to Joe Gordon and said, 'Here, Joe, you tag him.' Brother, that was really piling it on."

Baseball, you can readily see, is a serious game—but not always.

QUICKIES FROM HARRY HERSHFIELD:

The gal who saw her first baseball game and gave her opinion: "I like the pitcher the best—he hit the bat every time."

In the bleachers they had to contend with a jumping, fist waving, and shouting dame yelling: "Kill the umpire—kill the umpire." "Pipe down," said one neighbor, "he ain't done nothing wrong." "That's what you think—he's my husband—kill the umpire."

Of the goof who applied as player on a team. He said he would be a sensation and would be the biggest draw they ever had. He said he could hit home runs with his head. The manager, however, wanted to get a sample first. The goof went to the plate and the pitcher let him have a fast one. He hit it right flush with a swing of his head, sending the ball out over the bleachers. But he never played on the team. For a guy with a white coat came and took him away and explained to the manager: "He'd hit that ball every time—he's got bats in his belfry."

The Phantom Phee-nom of Coogan's Bluff

BY JIM MCCULLEY

Clint Hartung was a baseball legend even before he came to the major leagues. Probably no player in the history of the game—certainly none in the era which takes in the last three decades—hit the big time with more fanfare, more expected of him, than Clinton Clarence Hartung, born August 10, 1922, in Hondo, Texas.

A 6-foot, 4-inch, 225-pound stalk of steellike muscle and strength, Hartung, of German descent, made his debut with the New York Giants in the spring of 1947. They weren't sure whether Clint was going to develop into another Christy Mathewson, a right-handed Babe Ruth, or both. Such was the magnitude of his accomplishments in high school, a

103

season in class D, and almost four years of service baseball.

Hartung was a publicity man's dream come true. And Garry Schumacher, former New York *Journal-American* baseball writer turned tub thumper for the Giants, pulled out all the stops in announcing the arrival, at last, of baseball's Paul Bunyan.

Schumacher, a knowledgeable man of the trade and one of the writing fraternity's greatest wits then as he is now, struck on a descriptive phrase about the Hartung situation which shall always remain a classic in the sport: Garry, extending his long arms to the heavens and his throat vibrant with uncontrolled enthusiasm, shouted: "He's a sucker for showing up. He should go straight to the Hall of Fame at Cooperstown."

But who could challenge that statement by the "Governor," as his intimates call Schumacher? For the Giants had purchased the contract of Hartung for $25,000 and four players sight unseen, from wise old Mike Kelly of Minneapolis, more than a year before.

Kelly came to know Hartung by coincidence, actually. While Mike's Minneapolis team was training at New Braunfels, Texas, in the spring of 1942, Clint was pitching and playing the outfield for Hondo High School not too far away. Hartung's principal brought the youngster to Kelly and on the strength of one look Mike signed the kid.

After leaving high school Hartung was sent to Eau Claire in the Wisconsin State League. In 66 games that season, he hit for an average of .358, clouting 12 homers, and accounted for a total of 120 runs scored and batted in. Before the year was out Clint was in the Army Air Force, based at Hondo.

He played ball in the service, naturally, and his diamond feats were astounding. The Giants were all set to welcome

104

the youngster to camp in the spring of '46, but Hartung decided to remain in the Air Force for another year. He was shipped to Hickam Field, Honolulu. And the Hartung story grew bigger, and bigger.

Before Hartung reported to the Giants in '47, the late Mel Ott, then manager of the team, received a letter from a Major Clayton Heinlen. It read:

"As catcher-member of the Hickam baseball team, Honolulu, I would like to tell you the record of one of your newly acquired players. . . . Clint Hartung was member of my team that won 67 games and lost four this season. . . . Hartung pitched 25 games and lost none, averaging 15 strikeouts a game. . . . He also played in the outfield, hitting for an average of .567. . . . He also hit 30 home runs and cut off numerous runs at the plate with throws from deep left field. . . . Clint will be reporting to the Giants' spring training camp in February."

The Giants had purchased Hartung's contract from Kelly on the advice of Mike himself.

"Hartung is the greatest prospect I've seen in my fifty years of baseball," Kelly had told his friend and owner of the Giants, Horace Stoneham.

And at the winter meetings of '46 in Los Angeles, with the Giants anticipating Hartung's release from service, Clint's name hit the headlines again. They were made from quotes on Clint by Ted McGrew, then chief scout for the Boston Braves.

"That kid is a whole baseball club by himself," said McGrew, who had wanted Clint for the Braves. "He can hit the ball from county to county and he can play anywhere. He's a pitcher, an outfielder and a first baseman, all in one."

So it was that Clint Hartung came to the Giants—already known as the "Hondo Hurricane" for his prodigious feats. It wasn't long before Clint became "Floppy" to his Giant teammates for his big ears, his loping mannerisms, and his friendly St. Bernard nature.

During the spring training season of '47, at Phoenix, the nicknames fit him to a tee. Nobody was ever seen to hit a ball farther than the Hondo Hurricane in the desert regions of the great Southwest, and his lovable, modest nature won him friends wherever he went, among the players, writers, and fans.

Maybe Schumacher was right; maybe the kid should go right to the Hall of Fame. But all Hartung did was smile and say: "Wait till I strike out a few times. They'll forget all about me and I'll be back in the bushes."

Clint couldn't have know how prophetic his words were to be. Because of his tremendous power at the plate, the Giants forgot about him as a pitcher. He started the season in left field, but despite his apparent power, he became a menace to the club and himself in the outfield. Three weeks after the season started Ott had to bench him.

All of a sudden this truly great physical specimen became a burden and an enigma. Such were the rules of the game that he could not be farmed out for more seasoning without obtaining waivers on him, and his potential was so great that the Giants knew they could not get the necesssary waivers. So Clint sat around, pinch hitting, pinch running occasionally, and pitching batting practice.

Then the night of May 9, 1947, with the Braves in the Polo Grounds, and holding a big early-inning lead, Ott turned around to Hartung and said: "You, go to the bullpen." Clint looked around to see whom Mel was talking to. "You, I mean," said Mel, pointing to Hartung.

Clint wasn't in the bullpen more than a couple of minutes when he got a call to go to the mound to start the fourth

106

inning. What next transpired was unbelievable, and made one of the more inspiring stories of the '47 season: one—two—three—four—five—six innings of shutout ball, no runs, no hits, and five strikeouts.

Well, if he couldn't be another Babe Ruth, perhaps he was another Christy Mathewson. Hartung joined the Giants starting staff. He ran off a string of four straight victories before losing to Bucky Walters of the Reds.

Once his streak—29 games counting his service wins—was broken, Hartung finished the '47 season with 9 games won, 7 lost, and a batting average of .309. The Giants had more than reclaimed their $25,000.

Hartung remained a pitcher for the next two years, compiling an 8 and 8 record in '48 and a 9 and 11 mark in '49. He was blazing fast, but they couldn't teach him to throw a curve, and a fast ball is not enough in the major leagues. The '50 season saw Hartung pitch only occasionally, play a few times in the outfield and a few times at first base. That year he was 3–3 on the mound and hit .302. Clint had just about had it, but he lasted two more years with the Giants, as a pinch hitter and a pinch runner, because he was still very fast afoot. In '51, the year of the Miracle pennant, Clint hit .205 in 21 games; the following year, his last in the majors, he batted .218 in 28 games.

Hartung, who had come to the big leagues with trumpets blaring six years earlier, went out with a lifetime major league batting average of .212 and stood 29–29 as a pitcher.

Clint played a little minor league ball after that but he couldn't stand it. He went home and got a job in an oil refinery at Sinton, Texas.

He last hit the national headlines in the fall of '57. Said a story out of Wichita, Kansas:

"Clint Hartung's two-run homer in the ninth inning won

the National Non-Pro baseball title last night for the Sinton Oilers. It was his third round-tripper of the tournament. Hartung batted .457 in the seven games as Sinton rolled unbeaten to the title.

"When Hartung lifted that 415-foot homer over the center-field fence last night, he circled the bases grinning."

A scene typical of the Hondo Hurricane:

It is not hard to visualize Hartung's grin. He was always grinning, good times or bad, except maybe once.

It was maybe '51 or '52. Clint's golden bubble was shattered by this time and he was definitely on the way out. But he was still good copy, and Bill Roeder, then covering the Giants for the *World-Telegram and Sun,* wrote a spring training piece about Floppy. It was syndicated and distributed to papers all over the Scripps-Howard chain. It recalled the Hartung feats of yore, and ended up by saying, in so many words, "Well, maybe the Hondo Hurricane has blown out to sea, but Clint Hartung is still the best darn pinball player in the major leagues," which he was.

Everywhere the Giants went barnstorming that spring, Roeder's piece appeared in the local bugle, saved by the editor for the day the Giants arrived in town.

Clint thought Bill was writing a Hartung baseball obit every day. Finally, Hartung could stand it no longer. One afternoon he dashed up to Leo Durocher, the local paper in hand, and demanded of the manager: "How much will it cost me to punch a reporter in the nose?" Durocher almost fell off the bench laughing. Nobody had ever seen Hartung mad before. Roeder ducked him for the rest of the trip.

IV. It Happened to a Pitcher

Baseball fans are given to speculation about what goes on in mound conferences during tense moments in the national pastime. Many years ago I made it a point to find out after a huddle between Lefty Gomez, the great Yankee pitcher, and Tony Lazzeri, his second base teammate. With the bases loaded and no one out, Lazzeri called for time and walked to the pitcher's box. He looked Gomez squarely in the eye and said:

"You got yourself into this; get yourself out!"

Gomez relaxed in laughter and did pitch himself out.

JIM FARLEY

This was during spring training in 1961 and after the Yankees had finished their workout, Ralph Terry and Ryne Duren went out for a round of golf with a pair of sports writers.

Terry "let out a little shaft" on the eighteenth hole and his tee shot wound up in a deep gully among some rocks near a brook.

A TOOTH FOR A TOOTH!   BURRIS JENKINS JR.

Trying to be sympathetic as they walked toward the site, one of the writers consoled Terry:

"Don't worry, Ralph, you're not in such bad shape."

"Yeah," muttered the disgusted Terry, "I'm fine, but how about my ball?"

LEO PETERSON

One of the first American Indians to play in the majors was Ed Pinnance, a pitcher who reported to the Athletics in 1903 with a suitcase made from the skin of an elk he had shot with a bow and arrow. He was immediately nicknamed "Peanut."

"I don't mind," he said. "I'll be roasted probably, but doesn't roasting usually improve peanuts?"

Pinnance had been discovered by Harry Davis, veteran Athletic player, while taking the baths at Mount Clemens, Michigan.

LEE ALLEN

110

No one ever had more fun on a ball field than Al Schacht, rightfully called the "Clown Prince of Baseball," who has entertained untold thousands all over this country and wherever our soldiers, sailors and marines have pulled duty. His talents as a comedian were not developed overnight but through the years when he was pitching for the Washington Senators or for the several minor league clubs he served. Even during a game this zany overlooked no opportunity to enjoy himself and make others laugh.

Reading, which was in the International League, was one of Al's stopovers in the twenties and one day his team was playing a double-header in Baltimore. To amuse the fans between games, Al played a hilarious "round of golf" with a ten-cent baseball, using a fungo stick for a club. When the show was over, he put the stick back in the bat rack, stuck the ball in his shirt front and went to the bullpen. Reading took an early lead in the second game but the Orioles, one of the strongest minor league clubs ever seen, began to catch up and trailing in a late inning, had two men on the bases with none out.

"That," Al said, "was when I was called upon to put out the fire. On my way to the box I realized I had the dime ball still on me and when the catcher came out to meet me and hand me the regular ball, I told him:

" 'Stand close to me so the umpire can't see me very good,' which he did. I explained to him about the dime ball, which I was getting out of my shirt while I stuck the regular ball in there.

" 'When you catch this ball,' I told him, 'get it back to me as fast as you can. I don't want anybody to get a look at it.'

" 'You'll never get away with it,' he said.

" 'Maybe not,' I said, 'but it's worth trying and it may be worth a laugh.'

111

"By that time I had stuffed the real ball in my shirt and had the dime ball in my glove. The first hitter I pitched to was Joe Boley, the shortstop, who came up the next year with the Athletics. I gave him a fast ball, straight as a string, and he swung on it and popped it up a few feet from the plate and I yelled 'I got it!' because I didn't want anybody to get a close look at it. When I caught it, I saw it was flattened a little where Boley had hit it. I guess it was stuffed with sawdust. I rolled it in my hands to make it round again and now the hitter was Lena Stiles, the catcher. I gave him the same kind of pitch I'd given Boley and he smashed it— and popped it up, and I caught it.

"Now I had a hard time squeezing it back into shape but I managed it. Next was Rube Parnham, the pitcher but a good hitter, which was why Jack Dunn, the Baltimore manager, left him in the game instead of taking him out for a pinch hitter. He got the same pitch—and the same result, only this time the ball, instead of coming down straight, was dipping and twisting and lurching because it was all out of shape. Even as I was catching it, Parnham was screaming to the umpire, Bill McGowan:

" 'Look at the ball! Look at the ball!'

"McGowan said, 'Let me see that ball.'

"I knew the jig was up and I laughed and rolled it along the ground to him and it flopped over and over and everybody could see it and the crowd was in an uproar. I had to get out of it some way and when I saw McGowan didn't know what to do for the moment, I said:

" 'Look. I'll level with you. Parnham's the only one I pitched it to. I pitched the real ball to Boley and Stiles. Here it is.'

"When I pulled it out of my shirt and handed it to him, he was sore as hell and he asked me:

112

GOIN' ON RECORD

HONUS WAGNER'S 2,185 GAMES

MEL OTT'S 1,860 RBIs

HONUS WAGNER'S 3,430 HITS

MEL OTT'S 1,859 RUNS

5,778 TOTAL BASES

697 DOUBLES

5 HRs IN DOUBLE-HEADER

IF YOU HAVE A MIND FOR STATISTICS, HERE ARE SOME STAN MUSIAL CARRIES AROUND WITH HIM ALL THE TIME. THE OTHERS HE'LL LOAD UP WITH IN THIS, HIS 20TH SEASON!

113

" 'What are you trying to do? Make a joke of this game?'

"By this time Dunnie and all the Orioles were yelling at him, demanding that he do something about it but they didn't know what he should do and neither did he, so I said:

" 'Look. I got Boley and Stiles out with the real ball. Let me pitch to Parnham again.'

"The Orioles were still yelling but McGowan said:

" 'All right! All right! Get off the field and we'll get on with the game! Pitch to Parnham again, Schacht.'

"Parnham still was so mad I knew I could throw him anything and he would try to kill it. So I pulled the string on a fast ball and he swung from the heels—and popped it up and I caught it. Then I walked toward the plate and tossed the ball to him and said:

" 'There it is. Want to examine it?'

"By now he was so furious he threw the ball over the grandstand and McGowan not only threw him out of the game but fined him a hundred dollars, which an umpire in that league could do in those days."

F. G.

Warren Spahn could've become the first $100,000 salary pitcher in baseball. In 1952 the regular 20-game winner dipped to 14 and 19 for the seventh place Braves. Before he left for his Oklahoma farm at the end of the season, the club tried to sign him with a cut but he refused. To break the stalemate, they offered him a bonus deal of 10 cents on every admission over 800,000 during the 1953 season. Boston fans had soured on the Braves and an 800,000 figure looked far away. That winter the Braves suddenly shifted to Milwaukee and their admission total in their new surround-

115

ings for 1953 was 1,800,000. Had Spahn accepted the gimmick offer, he'd have received an extra $100,000.

F. G.

When Lefty Gomez was courting his lovely June O'Dea he took her to see her first ball game. Lefty lost a 1–0 decision and later June consoled him. "Don't worry, honey, you'll beat them tomorrow," she cooed. Gomez exploded: "Tomorrow? Who do you think you're marrying, Iron Man McGinnity?"

MAX KASE

At a banquet in Birmingham, Michigan, Paul Foytack was asked if Red Wilson was a good catcher.
"I dunno," said Foytack. "He never caught anything I threw. The batter always got to it first."

The Tigers were riding the team bus to Wrigley Field in Los Angeles. Jim Bunning was reading an account of Mickey Mantle's fiftieth homer.
"How about this guy?" said Bunning. "He hits one a day."
"Yeah," said Foytack, "he's just like a vitamin pill."

When the Tigers announced they were screening in the lower deck in right field of their Stadium to cut down on the number of home runs.
"Great," said Foytack. "What about the upper deck?"

JOE FALLS

The last couple of years they were together as a Yankee battery, Bill Dickey and Lefty Gomez worked without signs.
"He's so nearsighted he hardly can see a sign and even
116

if he does, he's likely to forget it," Bill explained. "So I look for a fast ball on every pitch and if I get a curve ball, it don't matter. If I looked for a curve ball and he let go with a fast one, I could get at least a broken finger."

RAY GRODY

Gomez was considerable of a wit in his own right. One day he and Red Ruffing, another Yankee pitching mainstay, came under the displeasure of Joe McCarthy, then manager of the Yankees, shortly after he had been elected to baseball's Hall of Fame. Gomez turned tables on his manager by an apt remark: "Red," he said, "between us we put McCarthy into the Hall of Fame."

JIM FARLEY

Waite Hoyt once said:
"A Yankee pitcher never should hold out because he might be traded and then he would have to pitch against them."
Waite was traded to the Tigers in 1931 and the first time he faced his old teammates they knocked him out of the box.

F. G.

Vernon (Lefty) Gomez, then with the Yankees, was pitching against the Red Sox and Jimmy Foxx was at bat, with one out, two on and the count 2 and 2. Bill Dickey, his catcher, gave him a sign and Lefty shook him off. Bill gave him another sign and, shaken off again, called time and walked out to the box.
"Just what do you want to throw him?" he asked.

117

"To tell you the truth," Lefty said, "I'd just as soon not throw him anything."

F. G.

Tony Lazzeri was at second base for the Yankees, Frankie Crosetti at shortstop, and Joe DiMaggio in center field. Lefty Gomez was pitching and the other club had a man on first base with one out. The hitter slapped a high bounder back to Gomez and the setup was perfect for a double play as Crosetti moved to cover second but Gomez unaccountably threw the ball to Lazzeri, who was at least twenty feet off the bag, and both runners were safe.

Lazzeri walked to the mound and asked Lefty:

"What the hell did you throw the ball to me for?"

"I've been hearing what a smart guy you are," Lefty said, "and I wanted to see what you'd do with that one."

Fortunately for Lefty, he got out of the inning without being scored upon, and when he went back to the dugout Joe McCarthy asked him mildly:

"Why did you throw the ball to Lazzeri?"

"I'll tell you, Joe. When I turned around I saw those two Dagoes. I didn't know which one to throw it to, so I threw it to the one closest to me."

And Joe said: "There was another one in center field. Why didn't you throw it to him?"

F. G.

William Dayton ("Pol") Perritt, who between 1912 and 1921 pitched for the Cardinals, the Giants and the Tigers, was a tall, lean, rather dour-looking man but there wasn't really anything dour about him. He was a first-rate pitcher—good enough to pitch and win a double-header, which he

118

did for the Giants against the Phillies at the Polo Grounds in 1916—but he was, in a nice way, one of baseball's most entertaining liars.

"I was pitching against Hans Wagner one day," he said, "and threw him a fast ball, right down the middle and he hit a line drive that, while I still was in my follow-through, went under my right arm and over the center-field fence."

And of his luck in the hunting field, he said:

"This was an especially good day for me. I was shooting and hitting everything that walked or flew. By the end of the day, when I was trudging home, I was so loaded down with birds, rabbits, squirrels and one small deer, that when I took a shot at a chipmunk high in a tree, the weight I was carrying bore me over backward just as I fired my gun. The shot wasn't wasted, though. I got a pheasant that had just took off in front of me."

F. G.

What kind of man was Walter Johnson? Well, this is Clyde Milan's story, told out of the time when Walter was pitching for the Senators and Clyde was a far-ranging outfielder and one of the greatest base stealers anybody ever saw:

"We were in Chicago and somebody had given us tickets to the theater. The service in the dining room was a little slow that night and we didn't have too much time to get to the show. As we started through the lobby a man stopped Walter. Walter didn't know him and I guessed all the man wanted was to shake his hand and tell him how much he admired him and I walked on a few feet and stood there, waiting for him, thinking he'd be on his way in a moment. But the man kept talking to him and I saw him nod a few

119

times and smile. I was getting fidgety, thinking we might miss the start of the show, but at last he shook hands with the man again and picked me up near the door.

" 'Who was that?' I asked him, and he said:

" 'I don't know. I never saw him before.'

" 'Then why did you spend so much time with him?'

" 'He said he knew my sister.'

" 'Your sister?' I said. 'I didn't know you have a sister.'

"And he said: 'I haven't. But he was such a nice man. I didn't have the heart to tell him so.' "

F. G.

There is one that concerns both Babe Ruth and Walter Johnson. On Ruth's first appearance in Washington after he began spraying home runs around the circuit, he faced Walter Johnson. The first pitch streaked across the plate. "Strike one," the umpire called. The second pitch was another sizzler. "Strike two," the umpire pronounced. The Babe set himself but the third pitch plunked into the catcher's mitt. "Strike three," called the umpire, "you're out." Ruth went to the umpire to ask, "Did you see any of those pitches?" "Nope," said the umpire truthfully. "Neither did I," Ruth confessed, "but that last one sounded kinda high to me."

JIM FARLEY

There is a year missing from Dizzy Dean's major league record—missing because he wasn't in the majors that year, although he should have been.

The year was 1931 and he was twenty years old. The Cardinals had brought him up from their Houston farm near the close of the 1930 season, more to look at him than anything else, because they were winning the pennant and they really didn't need him. But they carried him around for a couple of weeks, and on the last day of the season he was tossed in against the Pirates. He was a raw kid, a scant year out of the Regular Army and had divided the season between St. Joe in the Western League and Houston in the Texas, but in that first big league start, he shut the Pirates out, yielding only three hits, two of them scratches.

Now the Cardinals were heading for the World Series with the Philadelphia Athletics and Sam Breadon, who owned the club, asked Diz if he would like to go with them as a spectator, since he was not eligible as a player, not having been in the league long enough.

"Do I get paid?" Diz asked.

"No," Breadon said, "but I'll take care of all your expenses."

"The hell with it," Diz said, "I'll wait until I pitch in one. I'll enjoy that more."

The following spring at Bradenton, where the Cardinals trained, Diz was the big noise. Figuratively and literally. He unloosed more stuff than any young pitcher the club had seen in many a day, he had all the regular hitters waving in the breeze, and all any reporter who visited the camp could write about or talk about was Dizzy Dean.

He grabbed all the headlines. Grabbed them? He made them, either by pitching or by just talking about it. He was the gabbiest guy to come up from the minors in all the years anybody could remember, full of wind and having a very high opinion of himself. The National League? That was a joke to him. Remember what he did to the Pirates last fall? That was just a sample. He'd win twenty-five games, maybe thirty. The Cardinals had some pretty good hitters, such as Jim Bottomley, Frank Frisch, Taylor Douthit and Chick

121

Hafey. Come on, let's see you hit this one! Ha! Ha! So you're the great Hafey!

If he'd had less stuff, the chances are the veterans would have chased him out of the camp, but he had so much it was a cinch he would be a winning pitcher in the National League. He took it for granted that he wouldn't have to go back to the minors again. But he did. Breadon, Branch Rickey, Gabby Street, the manager, and the others couldn't stand the gaff any longer. So back he went—and left them, laughing, when he said good-by. That is, he was doing the laughing. He figured the joke was on the Cardinals.

He reported to the Houston club in Dallas, arriving at noon, climbed into his uniform, and shut the home club out. The Texas League played a split season and his pitching won both halves of it for Houston as he racked up twenty-six victories. In a game with San Antonio he had eighteen strikeouts—and, across the season, a total of 303. One Sunday he pitched—and won—a double-header with Fort Worth. He rested on Monday and returned to the box on Tuesday to win the game that clinched the pennant.

The next spring, naturally, he was back with the Cardinals to start a string of five great seasons before an injury suffered in the All-Star Game in 1937 started him on the way to a swift decline. When it was all over, he must have looked back with longing wonderment to the missing year when he, who belonged in the majors, was toiling under the Texas sun.

F. G.

O. Henry once wrote a story called *Roads of Destiny* in which a young shepherd poet named David had to die, no matter which way he took when he came to a fork in the road

122

to Paris, by a pistol bearing the crest of the Marquis de Beaupertuys. . . .

Once there was a young left-handed pitcher by the name of John Benton who came out of Clinton, North Carolina. That was way back in 1910 and he pitched for the Macon club of the South Atlantic League and he was so good that before the season was over he was sold to Cincinnati. The Reds farmed him out to Chattanooga the next year and recalled him in the fall and two years later he was one of the best pitchers in the National League and a hero in Cincinnati. Rube Benton, they were calling him by that time, and he still was just a kid at heart. If he hadn't been he wouldn't have gone scooting around the town by night on a motorcycle, risking his neck, to say nothing of his pitching arm. But that was his idea of pleasure and, night after night, he went roaring over the seven hills on which Cincinnati is built.

One night he came roaring out of a side street into a broad avenue. His view of the avenue was obscured by shrubbery on a corner, and he didn't see a car that was going at high speed, too, until it was too late and he smashed into it. When they picked him out of the tangled wreckage of his motorcycle, they thought he would not live to pitch another ball game. He did, though. They carried him off to a hospital, removed pieces of his motorcycle from him, and laid his broken body on a bed and after a while he recovered, although he bore many scars, especially on his face and neck.

Within an incredibly short time he was pitching again. He won 150 games in the majors for the Reds and the Giants and for five years after he went back to the minors he was the best pitcher in the American Association. So he went around and about, happy and carefree, enjoying his

123

work and the money he made, having friends everywhere his schedule took him. He'd never been to school, never even learned to read or write, but he found his lack of education no bar to his happiness.

The last time his name appeared in the newspapers was in December of 1937. The dispatch was from Dothan, Alabama, and it began:

"John C. ('Rube') Benton, former major league pitcher, died here this morning of injuries suffered at Ozark last night in an automobile accident."

F. G.

One of the feats for which Walter Johnson is famous was that of pitching three shutouts against the Highlanders, as the Yankees were called in that era, in one series at the old Hilltop grounds in New York in 1908.

"Most people think I did it in three days," Walter once said, "but it was four days. We played Friday and Saturday but we couldn't play on Sunday because there was no Sunday baseball in New York then, so we had to lay over until Monday.

"It was a funny thing about those games. They said I pitched them to help the other fellows out. I didn't. I couldn't help myself. I pitched the first game and on Saturday a newspaperman asked Joe Cantillon, our manager, who was going to pitch for him and he said:

" 'Johnson is going good. I think I will pitch him today.'

"So I pitched that game and on Monday there was a double-header and before the first game the same newspaperman came down and asked Joe who was going to pitch and Joe said:

" 'Well, that Johnson is still going good. I guess I'll pitch him.'

"When that game was over I went to the clubhouse and hid out until the second game had gone a few innings. I was just a big, dumb kid and I said to one of the fellows:

" 'I believe that Mr. Cantillon is playing a joke on me.' "

JIMMY DURANTE

Bobo Newsom, the pitcher, used to get excellent mileage out of his winter salary debates with the late Clark Griffith, also with Connie Mack. At one point when Mr. Mack reacted to Newsom's ravings about the miserliness of the Athletics, commenting kindly that "Newsom's just a big overgrown boy," Bobo retorted, "Maybe so, but I want a grown man's salary."

When Newsom was with the Senators, and going into his annual holdout act against Griffith, it used to be the habit of Washington baseball writers motoring south to make Hartsville, South Carolina, an overnight stop. This was for the purpose of ascertaining Newsom's latest state of mind on salary matters.

Besides, Hartsville was a convenient stop on what used to be a boring three-day auto trip to Florida, enlightened only by the roadside musings of the poet laureate of Burma Shave. This was where Bob Considine found himself one year and he hied to Newsom's home for the customary interview on the pitcher's holdout and his threat to stay away from training camp.

"When you get to Florida, tell Griffith I won't sign for what he's offering until hell freezes over," Newsom told Considine. "Tell that old goat I'll sit here all summer." This was the substance of Considine's report to his newspaper. Two days later, when he pulled up into Orlando, Griffith met him

125

in the lobby. "Newsom's signed contract just came in the air mail today. Thought you ought to know," Griffith said.

SHIRLEY POVICH

In 1931 Johnny ("Grandma") Murphy, who later became one of the all-time great relief pitchers with the Yankees, was starting his professional baseball career with the Newark Bears.

I had met John when he was a Fordham star, so I took my little nine-year-old nephew, a spoiled kid to put it mildly, to see my friend pitch against Rochester in the second game of a double-header at Newark Stadium.

The kid, Billy Post was his name (and it still is), was not content just to see a ball game. "Can't we sit on the bench? I thought you said you knew him! These are lousy seats!"

My name-dropping honor was at stake. "C'mon," I said, "we'll go down between games. I'll have you meet him."

So down under the stands and to the dugout we went. Without too much fuss we got to Johnny. He put it on good. Acted like it was me who taught him to pitch. He even went further. "I'll get young Bill a ball." He somehow wheedled one out of the manager. These were depression days, remember. Also he borrowed a fountain pen and very graciously autographed the ball and presented it to Bratty Billy.

I waited for the "Gosh! Thanks! Wow!" but it didn't come. Instead the kid very condescendingly gave out with "My father got me a Babe Ruth autographed ball, a Ty Cobb, and a Lou Gehrig . . . but . . ." (and here he tossed John's gift in the air a few times) "me and the other guys can play with this one."

BOB DUNN

A rookie pitcher kept begging the manager for a chance to start a game. His day finally came, but the rookie pitcher was knocked out in the first inning. The manager took the youngster aside and told him he was being given his release.

"But won't you give me a recommendation?" pleaded the boy.

"Sure," the manager replied and wrote the following: "Joe Doaks pitched one game for me and I'm satisfied!"

LES BIEDERMAN

The baseball anecdote I seem to think of more than any other concerns a marine sergeant who served with me in the 2nd Marine Division during World War II.

He was a proud Indian from the state of Washington and came off the same reservation that sent Bob and Roy Johnson to the major leagues. He was known as "Chief" McGaa. He claimed to have pitched pro ball in the Northern League

127

as well as the Northwestern League, I believe, before the war.

The Chief constantly bragged about his talents and that he was a pitcher. But the men in the 18th Regiment, to which he was attached, always "rode" him about it. Even after the day he pitched five hitless innings in the first baseball game ever played in New Zealand in 1943, where the 2nd Marine Division was stationed.

Finally, the Chief decided he would produce official proof that he was a pitcher. He wrote his mother and asked her to send him the Official Baseball Guide of 1942.

The book arrived some months later, after the division had invaded Tarawa. When it came, the Chief went around to his "ribbers"—of whom I was one—and proudly opened the book, pointed to a list of pitching records at the end of which was listed: "McGaa, Tacoma, Won 2, Lost 17." And as he showed it, with great flourish and personal satisfaction, he said, "Didn't I tell you, I was a pitcher?"

HY HURWITZ

SATCHEL PAIGE'S "HOW TO STAY YOUNG":

1. Avoid fried meats, which angry up the blood.
2. If your stomach disputes you, lie down and pacify it with cool thoughts.
3. Keep the juices flowing by jangling around gently as you move.
4. Go very light on the vices, such as carrying on in society. The social ramble ain't restful.
5. Avoid running at all times.
6. Don't look back. Something might be gaining on you.

LAWTON GARNER

128

Joe Engel, president of the Chattanooga club, once pitched for Clark Griffith in Washington. He was good, but very wild. It wasn't a question of whether Engel could get the ball over the plate but whether he could keep it in the ball park.

Griffith finally called Engel into the office to tell Joe he was being sent to Minneapolis.

"For whom?" Engel asked.

"For nobody," Griffith replied. "It's an even trade and it will strengthen our ball club!"

LES BIEDERMAN

V. It Happened in the Infield

Johnny Logan, former Brave and now with Pittsburgh, was accosted by a stranger who asked if Johnny remembered him.

"I remember the name," he said, "but I can't *replace* the face."

RAY GRODY

"Baseball is like this," Frank Frisch says. "Have one good year and you can fool them for five more, because for five more years they expect you to have another good one."

From Al Rosen: "The greatest thrill in the world is to end the game with a home run and watch everybody else walk off the field while you're running the bases on air."

F. G.

Frankie Frisch, the Old Flash, tells this story on himself: "When I had a television sports program I was asked to pick an all-time, all-Major League club. After naming the Wagners, Cobbs, Mathewsons, Alexanders, Ruths and all the other greats, I sat back in my chair and said: 'Ah! How I would love to manage a team like that! I'd fire up a big fat cigar and just watch 'em with pleasure!'

"I had no sooner said this than three advertising agency men blew their gaskets. I couldn't blame them. I forgot I had a cigarette company as my sponsor."

F. G.

The seriousness with which Ty Cobb approached baseball was brought home to me in an exhibition game the Athletics played in New Haven in 1927 or 1928. Cobb was finishing up his career with the A's. Weiss Park, of course, was owned by George Weiss. In this particular exhibition game a young fellow named Al Simmons was playing center field and Cobb was in right. The New Haven batter hit a long drive to center. Simmons moved easily to his left to catch the ball for the out. However, to do a little clowning for the edification of the fans, Al simulated a muff, by letting the ball bounce up from the pocket of the glove as if he had fumbled it, but then catching it as it came down. This drew a gasp and then an appreciative laugh from the fans, who understood what Simmons was doing. Al threw the ball to the infield and then looked over toward Cobb in right, apparently for approval. He didn't get it. Ty made a deprecatory downward movement with his right hand, almost as if to say, "Don't be a busher."

That same day a red-cheeked youngster caught a few innings for the A's. He could not have been more than nineteen years old and he certainly looked good up at that plate. His name was Jimmy Fox, and I leave off the second *x* because, as I recall, the Weiss Park program that day billed him with only one.

Then there's the story which, perhaps, epitomizes the demanding and fickle nature of the Philadelphia fans. This one also involves Jimmy Foxx and we can now give him the second *x*. Foxx was more or less my favorite ballplayer of all time—and it is a great sadness to me that he has had such bad days since leaving the game.

Anyhow, in 1933 I drove all the way from New Haven, Connecticut, to Philadelphia to see the A's open their home season against Washington. Because of a mistake about starting time, the first inning was already under way and the A's were at bat when I parked my $110, 1928, four-door, green Chevrolet sedan on one of those little streets behind right field at Shibe Park. Running down Somerset Street, which was behind the left-field wall, I heard a great roar go up and saw a baseball come whistling over the double-decked tier into the parking lot across the street.

"I came over a hundred and fifty miles," I said, "to see Foxx hit a home run and now I've missed it by a couple of minutes."

I mentioned my bad luck to the ticket seller, but he said, "Never mind, kid, he'll probably hit another one."

The ticket seller was right. Walter Stewart, a sidearm left-hander (a breed of which Double X was deeply enamored) was pitching. In the sixth inning Foxx hit another home run over the double-deck roof. There was nobody on for this one; there had been two on for the first one. In the ninth inning with the bases full, James slashed a single through the wicket, to drive in two more runs. I believe he walked the other two times up. So he had three for three, six runs batted in, three or four runs scored, and the A's won 9–1.

However, in the ninth inning, with two out, Jimmy fumbled a little roller for an error, whereupon an Athletic rooter in my vicinity turned around and pontificated, "That's Foxx for you."

TIM COHANE

When Hank Greenberg was at his peak with the Tigers and terrorizing enemy pitchers with his home run blasts, someone asked him:

"When, in your own mind, did you become a major league ballplayer?"

"One day when we were playing the Yankees at the Stadium," Hank said. "Up to that time, I had dreaded playing in New York. I'd had an opportunity to sign with the Yankees and had rejected it for two reasons. One was that, as a first baseman, I knew I had no chance to make a place for myself as long as Lou Gehrig was around and I didn't want to spend years in the minor leagues waiting for him to slow down. The other was that, born and raised in the Bronx, I didn't want to look bad in my home town when I came in with the Tigers. There were days when I actually prayed for rain when we were scheduled there. When we played there I never wanted to have to go to bat in a pinch.

"But this day, there I was. With two out we were tied and Charlie Gehringer was the hitter. I followed him and, as I waited on deck, I found myself calling to him:

" 'Get on, Charlie! I'll bring you in!'

"Charlie doubled and I brought him in with a single. That was the day."

F. G.

Ty Cobb credits his teammates in Detroit with giving him the incentive to become the great player he was. When Cobb joined the Tigers, the other players gave him a rough time, as was the custom with rookies in those days.

They resented his freshness and they banded together to keep him from taking the place of one of the veterans. They tried to keep him from the batting cage and off the field; they wouldn't eat with him or room with him.

"I hated them as much as they hated me," Cobb later told the story, "but I'm grateful for what they did for me. They drove me off by myself and I ate alone, roomed alone and walked alone.

"What else could I do between dinner and bedtime? There were no movies when I started and if there were I wasn't aware of them. I couldn't go to a vaudeville show every night and I didn't want to hang out in pool parlors, bowling alleys and saloons. And I wasn't much of a reader.

"So I'd walk the streets for a couple of hours and this helped keep my legs in shape. Then I'd sit in my room or lie in bed and I had plenty of time to think. And what else was I to think about but baseball—how to hit pitchers, how to play for hitters, and how to run the bases."

LES BIEDERMAN

Gil Hodges turned down a steak dinner on a plane because it was Friday. A teammate, also a Catholic, advised him to have the steak, saying: "There's an automatic dispensation when you're on a plane and they're serving only that."

Hodges hedged. "That might be, but we're a little too close to headquarters up here," he said.

MAX KASE

134

FIRST TIME OUT! **By BILL GALLO**

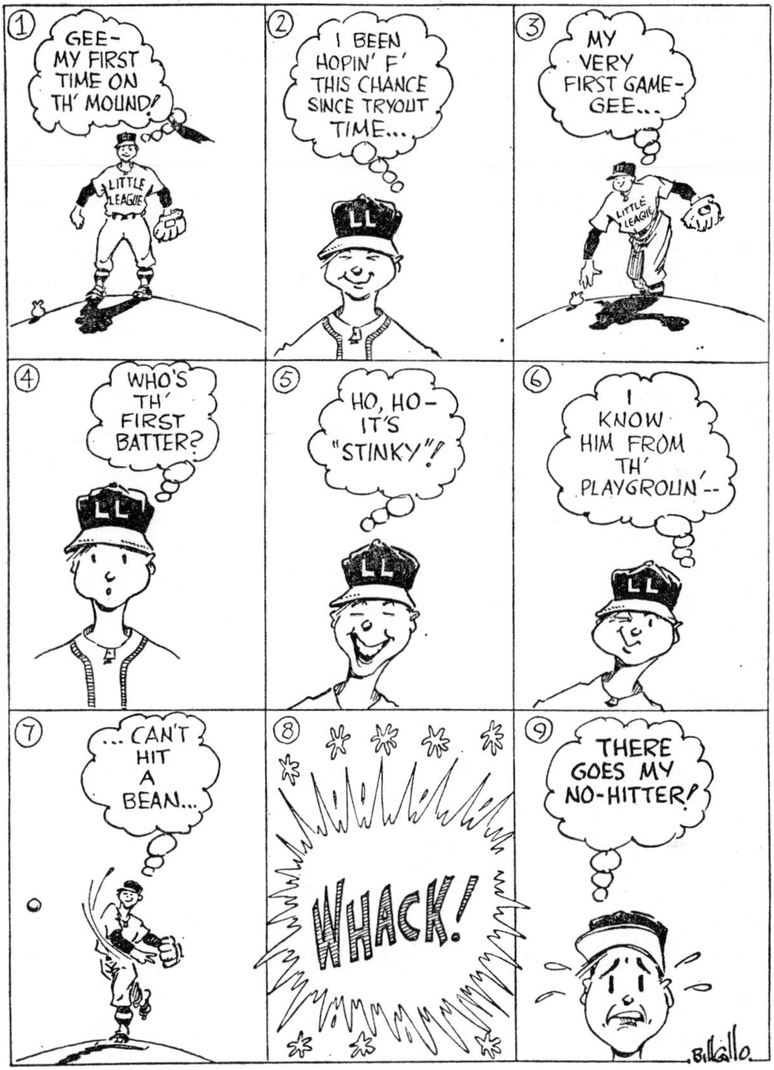

Not long before he signed off, the immortal Ty Cobb dropped in to see his friend Lawton Carver, newsman-restaurateur-sportsman. Cobb was very blue. After a couple of drinks he became bluer than blue.

"I haven't got a friend in baseball," he said, as tears began to come. "And you know why, Lawton. I cut 'em whenever they got in my way. I kicked them, I gouged them, I did everything to them—to win those ball games. Now look at me. Friendless, absolutely friendless."

Carver let him weep for a time, then said, "Ty, if you had your life to live over again would you do all those things?"

Cobb stopped the tears, blew his nose, glared at Lawton like an eagle and swore: "You're dam' right I would!"

BOB CONSIDINE

Back in 1919 when I was reporting the activities of the Minneapolis club of the American Association, the Millers did their spring training at Houston, Texas. And an important part of their training preparations was playing exhibition games with teams of the Texas League and Southern Association.

One weekend series was booked with the Galveston club of the Texas league. Strolling along the boardwalk skirting the Gulf of Mexico on Sunday morning after attending church with Joe Cantillon, colorful manager of the Millers, and Jack Lelivelt, who alternated at first base and right field, Lelivelt suddenly burst into laughter.

"Hey, Joe," exclaimed Lelivelt, "didn't we get Jimmy Smith from the Galveston club the last year you managed Washington in 1909?"

"Yeah," replied Cantillon, "quite a kid, wasn't he!" Then Joe began chuckling.

137

"What's the joke about Jimmy Smith?" I asked Cantillon. "Jack," said Joe to Lelivelt, "you tell Barton about Smith."

Lelivelt, by the way, after an eight-year career as an outfielder in the American League and two years with Minneapolis, later managed Milwaukee of the American Association and Los Angeles of the Pacific Coast league.

It's Jack Lelivelt's story from here on:

"In 1909, when I was playing for Joe at Washington, Clark Griffith, owner of the Nats, bought Jimmy Smith, a young third baseman, from Galveston. He was the cockiest kid to come up to the big show during my eight-year career in the American League.

"Young Smith boasted to all and sundry that he was the greatest third baseman in the history of baseball. He told veterans and youngsters alike on the Washington club; sports writers, hangers-on, in fact everybody who would listen to him, that compared to him, Jimmy Collins, who during his lengthy career with the Boston Red Sox was hailed as the greatest third sacker of his era, was just an ordinary guardian of the hot corner.

"Shortly after Smith joined the Nats, our regular third baseman, Germany Schaefer, became ill. This happened on the day we were opening a series with the Detroit Tigers headed by the one and only Ty Cobb.

"Cobb, in 1909, was playing his fifth season with the Tigers and already was hailed by virtually all baseball men and sports writers as being on his way to becoming the greatest baseball player, everything considered, in the history of baseball. Also, baseball's most fiery competitor.

"Managers and players on the American League's seven other clubs regarded Cobb as their most formidable individual threat at bat and on the bases. Once he got on base,

138

which seemed to be every time he came to bat, either by hitting safely or walking, Ty had players on the opposing team jumpy as a scared horse.

"With Schaefer out because of illness, Smith was getting his opportunity to prove his greatness as a third baseman.

"In the clubhouse before the game, Cantillon told Smith: 'Listen, kid, while I tell you how to play Cobb. He is a left-handed hitter, but he hits to all fields for he is in a class by himself as a place-hitter.

" 'You have to play Cobb in close because he is apt to lay a bunt down along the third-base line. When he does, bear in mind Cobb is fast as a streak. So, you have to pick up the ball and fire it to first base without setting yourself for the throw. Remember, if Cobb gets as much as a split second jump on you, he'll beat your throw to first base!'

"Instead of being impressed by Joe's advice, young Smith listened in a nonchalant manner. After Joe finished talking, Smith said:

" 'Don't worry, Joe, I'll take care of the great Cobb like he's never been taken care of before.'

"Well, the first time Cobb came to bat he laid down a bunt along the third-base line and was off like a streak of lightning to first base.

"Now, Smith, eager to make good his ability as a third baseman, charged in on the ball, all hands and feet. In his eagerness, he picked up dirt, grass and everything in sight except the ball.

"By the time Jimmy got his hands on the ball, Cobb had turned first base and was well on his way to second. Smith fired the ball blindly in the general direction of second base, but it went far into right field. Cobb easily beat the right fielder's throw to the plate.

"Out of the dugout came Cantillon to converse with

139

Smith, but before he could say anything, young Smith beat him to the punch by saying:

" 'Listen, Joe, don't get excited. You know this guy pitching today is using the spitball and I got hold of the wet side. Just wait until Cobb comes up the next time, and I'll show you how I'll handle him.'

"A few innings later, when Cobb again came to the plate, he decided to have some more fun with Smith. So, he laid down another bunt along the third-base line and again was off like a flash to first base.

"Now, Smith was all the more eager to make good his promise to Cantillon. He repeated his previous endeavors, but only more so. Jimmy grabbed everything in sight except the ball, and by the time he got his hands on the ball Cobb had rounded second base and was well on his way to third. So, Smith this time fired the ball in the general direction of second base and the ball went far into center field. Again, Cobb scored.

"Cantillon was really burned up. Out he came from the bench, cupped his hands and yelled so that everybody in the park could hear: *'Listen, punk, the next time Cobb comes to bat and lays a bunt down along the third-base line, never mind trying to throw him out at any base. Just grab the damned ball and run back to third base and try to head him off there!'* "

GEORGE A. BARTON

There was never any question as to "Who's on first?" when Hal Chase's name was in a line-up.

This incident explains why his dexterity as a fielder is legendary:

En route north after completing spring training, Chase and his team, the New York Highlanders, arrived at Athens,

140

Georgia, on March 13, 1910, for an exhibition game with the University of Georgia.

In the last half of the ninth inning, Chase tossed aside his first baseman's mitt, then took the shoe off his right foot and inserted his glove hand in the shoe. He accepted three chances!

"Prince Hal" was a more adept "glove man" with a spiked shoe than some of today's first sackers who use the oversized "lobster-claw" called a first baseman's mitt.

CLEM BODDINGTON

Someone pointed out a long time ago that when you are asked to pick an all-time, all-star team, it's best to start with shortstop because you pick Honus Wagner and you know nobody is going to knock down your choice, since there never has been another shortstop of Wagner's combined skills in the field and his power at bat. As a reflection of this way of thinking, there is the record of the original nominations for niches in the Hall of Fame at Cooperstown, called for in 1936, or three years before the Hall became a red-brick reality. Batches of candidates were submitted for every other position. Only Wagner was mentioned for shortstop.

Interesting, then, was the vote the Dutchman cast when he was asked whom he would like to have with him on his journey to immortality.

"Bill Terry on first base," he said. "Napoleon Lajoie on second, and Pie Traynor on third. Johnny Kling would be the catcher and Christy Mathewson and Cy Young would be the pitchers. In the outfield there would be Fred Clarke, Bill Lange, and Clarence Beaumont."

You might not agree with all his selections, but if he were around now to argue with you he would have this much going for him: He played with or against all save Traynor and Terry and, as a coach with the Pirates, he saw those Johnny-Come-Latelies regularly and at close range.

F. G.

Even the most alert and knowledgeable baseball men do not always recognize talent in the raw. The youthful Phil Rizzuto, before he was discovered for the Yankees by Paul Krichell, worked out at Ebbets Field for a couple of days when Casey Stengel was the Brooklyn manager but all he got from Casey was the brush. Many other players, including some of the great ones, have similar stories to tell. There was, for instance, a story going around about Pie Traynor when he was one of the all-time top third basemen. It was that Ed Barrow, then managing the Red Sox, had chased him out of Fenway Park. However, that wasn't—to put it mildly—quite accurate.

"I've heard it myself, many times," Pie said, "and I'm still trying to get it straightened out. Actually, I wasn't chased out of Fenway Park by Mr. Barrow. I was chased out of Braves Field by George Stallings.

"I was just out of high school in Somerville, Massachusetts, and a friend of mine told me he had arranged for me to work out with the Braves and I might make a good impression on Mr. Stallings. I took my glove and shoes to Braves Field and they gave me a uniform and I went out on the field. I didn't see Mr. Stallings but the Braves were taking batting practice and I went to third base and I was having a fine time, fielding the ball and throwing it around, when I heard somebody yell:

" 'Get out of there!'

"Then I saw it was Mr. Stallings, who had just come into the dugout, and he was glaring in my direction.

142

" 'Who, me?' I asked.

"And he yelled: 'Yes, you! Isn't it bad enough to be saddled with a ball club like this without having a clown like you tearing up the infield? Get off the field, take off that uniform, and don't come back!'

"I was so scared," Pie said, "I practically ran all the way home."

It was a couple of years before Stallings saw him again at Braves Field. George didn't recognize him. He was wearing the uniform of the Pirates.

F. G.

Most ballplayers know when they've reached the end of the high road. The less intelligent have to be told. For the bright ones, the certainty that they are through may come in a flash.

There was Joe McCarthy, manager and second baseman of the Louisville Colonels in 1921. It was his fifteenth year as a player and he had been aware for some time that he wasn't quite as good as he had been. Then came the day— and, as they say in bullfighting, the moment of truth. His first baseman was Jay Kirke, a powerful hitter but a clumsy, slow-thinking fielder, and they had a runner hung up between first and second.

"Jay had the ball," Joe said, "and was moving in on him. I yelled to him, 'Give me the ball! Give me the ball!' But he kept feinting. Suddenly the runner turned and raced toward me. I was still yelling but Jay still hesitated. Finally he made the throw. The runner charged into me and hit me in the chest with his shoulder and the ball hit me on the chin and down I went. When I got up I started to tell Jay what I thought of him but he stopped me cold:

143

" 'You know, Joe,' he said, 'you ain't looked too good to me yourself, lately.'

"That was it. I never played another game."

Leo Durocher, then managing the Brooklyn Dodgers and playing shortstop, got the sign in a game with the Reds in 1941. Ernest ("Botcho") Lombardi, surely the slowest man in baseball in his time, drilled a grounder to Leo.

"The ball came to me on a perfect hop," Leo said, "and I made a perfect throw to first base—but Lombardi beat it by a full step. In the clubhouse after the game, I said to the players:

" 'Get the scissors and cut the uniform off me. When I can't throw Lombardi out on a play like that, I've got to quit.'

"And," Leo said, "that's what I did."

Lefty Gomez had two good reasons for calling it a career.

"One," he said, "was that I was throwing as hard as I ever did but the ball wasn't going as fast as it had. The other was that it seemed to me some skulking reprobate had moved the plate back at least five yards."

F. G.

Like Joe DiMaggio and some of the other great all-around ballplayers, Jackie Robinson had the knack of lifting a sagging team and getting it back into the habit of winning. There was 1955, for instance, when the Brooklyn Dodgers got off to a tremendous start, then bogged down after the All-Star Game. Robinson, whose impressive play had helped them get the jump on their rivals early in the season, had to leave the starting line-up in July because of a leg injury.

144

In August the club was sluggish, and its followers began to have frightening visions of a collapse similar to the one that helped them blow a 13-game lead in 1951. Then, at the depth of their slump, Robinson returned to the line-up and was once more the frisky player he had been when he had come to the National League eight years before. Taking the extra base on hits, stealing second, third and home, beating out bunts, rattling enemy pitchers by dancing down off third, he was the spark that righted the Dodgers and allowed them to resume the drive toward their first world championship.

"My leg still bothers me," Jackie told a friend, "but the club has been playing dead ball and I thought I could put a little life into it."

Mission accomplished, Jackie then returned to the bench and concentrated on getting his leg in shape for what was to be his greatest World Series.

Robinson, like most of the better competitors, was as fiery and aggressive off the field as he was on it. He came to a friend in the Dodger clubhouse one day and showed him a clipping from a small New Jersey weekly newspaper.

"Read what this says about me," Jackie fumed. "I don't mind being knocked, but what this fellow says just isn't *true*."

The friend read the article and then handed it back to Jackie. "Of course, it isn't true," he said, "but it's a small paper and it isn't worth getting excited about."

"Well, I'm going to write this fellow a letter right now," Jackie said. "I'm going to set the record straight."

"Don't," his friend insisted. "The guy will just reprint your letter, which will make a big man out of him in that town, and he'll probably knock you again anyway."

"I can't help it," Jackie said. "I'm going to write him a letter."

He found a pen and a sheet of paper in the clubhouse and drafted a letter.

"What do you think of this?" he asked his friend.

"It's a good letter," his friend said, "but I wouldn't send it."

"Well, I'll hold it overnight and think about it," Jackie said.

When the friend came into the clubhouse the next day he saw Robinson and asked him about the letter.

Jackie grinned sheepishly. "I sent it," he admitted. "I just couldn't let the fellow get away with it—even if I *do* make a big man out of him."

FRANK GRAHAM, JR.

Ferris Fain, first baseman of the Philadelphia Athletics in the latter days of Connie Mack as manager, had read about the almost legendary skills of Hal Chase as a first baseman and one play that Chase made every once in a while particularly impressed him: With a runner on second base and none out (this was in the days when "inside baseball" was the vogue), the batter would lay down a sacrifice bunt toward third base to pull the third baseman off the bag and clear the way for the runner to romp down to third; Chase, having figured the play, would race across in front of the pitcher, scoop up the ball and fire it to the third baseman to make the putout.

Fain decided that at the first opportunity he would emulate Chase—and he did, but only to a degree. His strategy caught the third baseman napping and the throw went into left field, with the result that the runner coming down from second base scored and the batter reached second.

"Why did you throw the ball away?" Connie asked him when the inning was over.

Fain, still seething over the small disaster he had wrought, blurted:

"What did you expect me to do, eat it?"

Connie shrugged.

"Maybe it would have been better if you had," he said.

F. G.

The most famous, although surely not the best, double play combination was that of Joe Tinker at shortstop, Johnny Evers on second base, and Frank Chance on first for the Cubs, all three of them now enshrined at Cooperstown. Unknown to the public in the time of their greatness (1906–1908) was that Tinker and Evers so hated each other and savaged each other for misplays that Chance, who managed the club and could lick anybody on it, constantly had to keep them from coming to blows. Ultimately the enmity between them reached a point where they spoke to each other only on the field, and that's the way it was when they parted.

Someone asked Evers, following Tinker's death in retirement, if they'd ever become friends again and Johnny said:

"Yes—and most unexpectedly, about two years ago. I was in Chicago and was asked to take part in a radio salute to Chance on the anniversary of his passing and as I entered the studio I saw Joe for the first time in years. Neither of us knew the other was to be there and at the sight of each other, we had that old feeling again—meaning we wanted to fight. We started toward each other—and what do you think happened? When we got within punching distance we threw our arms around each other and cried like a couple of babies.

"Now Joe's gone, too, God rest him. I'm glad he left me as a friend."

F. G.

When Rocky Marciano was heavyweight champion of the world he told, with stars in his eyes, of having met Yogi Berra.

"What a great fellow he is!" Rocky said. "Nothing swelled-headed about him! Why, talking to him was just like talking to one of the fellows in the neighborhood."

When this was repeated to Yogi, he shook his head in disbelief. Assured that it was true, he said:

"How about that? And him the heavyweight champ! I felt the same way about him as he told you he felt about me. Why? I'm only a ballplayer. He's the *champeen* of the world."

"Maybe," Bill Heinz said, "it's because you made it as a catcher in the big leagues and he didn't."

"He ever try?" Yogi asked.

"Yes. He had a trial with one of the Cubs' farm clubs one spring but lasted only a couple of days. That's when he decided to become a fighter."

"Well," Yogi said, "he hits pretty good in that league, don't he?"

F. G.

Clyde McCullough was catching for the Pirates one day when a foul tip nicked him on the right hand. Mac should have retired but the Bucs were short of catchers and he had to stay on the job. The Giants sensed that McCullough had trouble gripping the ball and they began to steal.

Every time McCullough tried to catch a runner, he

149

threw high and the fielder had to jump for the ball. In one inning three Giants stole on Clyde and each time the throw came in high. When the inning ended, Eddie Bockman turned to McCullough and with a grin said, "Mac, they're sliding into third base, not flying in!"

LES BIEDERMAN

The awkward days of his earliest years with the Yankees were far, far behind him and Yogi Berra was playing to the hilt his role of elder statesman in the Yankee clubhouse. Rookies gathered around the great man as he sat majestically in front of his locker, dropping pearls of wisdom into their eager and receptive ears.

Yogi was telling the kids of his own experiences as a rookie. In the background floated Pete Sheehy, the clubhouse man, with an amused grin on his Irish face and the glint of a leprechaun in his eye.

"I wuz still in the Navy the first time I came in here," related Yogi, "and I wuz still wearin' my sailor uniform."

Suddenly he turned to Sheehy.

"Betcha never thought I looked like a ballplayer. Eh, Pete?" said Yogi.

"You didn't even look like a sailor," said Pete.

ARTHUR DALEY

On one of his annual swings through the training camps for his sports goods firm, Lefty Gomez measured the Yankees for uniforms. "What's your cap size?" he asked Yogi Berra.

"How do I know?" Yogi replied. "I'm not in shape yet."

MAX KASE

151

His teammates, the men who knew Roy Campanella best, used to call him "The Good Humor Man." He delivered his corny jokes and homey philosophy in a high-pitched voice that delighted his listeners. His humor was apt to break out at any time. During one important game, Roy was catching his roommate, Don Newcombe. He signaled for a fast ball but, for some reason, Newk threw a slow curve instead. Campy ambled out to the mound, scowled at Newk, and asked in a high voice:

"Hey, roomie, how come you throw me the local when I called for the express?"

Like all good-natured men Campy was the object of his colleagues' humor, too. They poked fun at him about his weight, about the mustache he usually showed up with at spring training, and about his age. They suspected that Roy, taking a leaf from Jack Benny's book, always gave himself the best of it when asked how old he was.

The liquor store he owned in Harlem came in for its share of kidding, despite the fact that Roy was not much of a drinker himself. During batting practice one day the Dodger players looked up into the stands at a fist fight which was in progress between a couple of fans.

"Hey, Campy," Gil Hodges shouted, "it looks like a couple of your customers are going at it up there."

"No, sir," Campy piped, shaking his head vigorously. "I don't sell any of that fighting liquor. I just sell *happy* liquor."

MAX KASE

152

VI. It Happened in the Outfield

The day before the 1926 World Series between the Yankees and the Cardinals opened, the Yanks were taking batting practice at the Stadium when there was an urgent telephone call for Babe Ruth. Urgent? A child was ill . . . and the Babe could help.

In Essex Fells, New Jersey, an eight-year-old boy named Johnny Sylvester slowly was convalescing from a serious illness. Too slowly, his doctor thought. What he needed desperately was a mental pickup. But from where? From whom?

"Johnny's a baseball fan," his father told the doctor. "His hero is Babe Ruth."

"That's it!" the doctor said. "Call the Babe and tell him . . ."

"But I don't know the Babe," his father said.

"I don't either," the doctor said, "but from what I've heard of him, it doesn't make any difference. I'm sure if you called him and explained . . ."

Now this was Johnny's father calling the Babe and the Babe listened and asked:

"Where do you live?"

"Essex Fells, New Jersey."

"How do you get there? . . . Yes. . . . Yes . . . Turn right at Route. . . . Then left . . . And there I am. All right. I'll be there this afternoon. But don't tell him I'm coming."

That afternoon the Babe was there, with an autographed ball, a bat and a glove. He sat at Johnny's bedside for an hour or more, answering his questions, telling him stories. And, of course, Johnny got well.

The Yankees opened the 1927 season in Philadelphia and the Babe, leaving the Hotel Adelphia for the ball park, stopped to talk to a couple of baseball writers in the lobby. As they talked, an elderly man came up and said:

"Mr. Ruth, I'm Johnny Sylvester's uncle."

"Glad to know you, sir," the Babe said. "How's Johnny?"

"Oh, he's fine now—thanks to you."

"I'm glad to hear that, sir," the Babe said.

"We can't ever express our gratitude to you," the man said. "But I want you to know that we'll never forget what you did for him. I didn't mean to interrupt you and these other gentlemen but I did want to be able to tell Johnny I saw you and talked to you and I know he'll be glad."

"Fine!" the Babe said. "Give Johnny my regards."

As the man walked away, the Babe said to his friends:

"Who the hell is Johnny Sylvester?"

"The little sick boy you went to see in Essex Fells last fall."

"Oh, sure," the Babe said. "I remember now."

A Babe Ruth story. There are, as Jimmy Durante would say, a million of them. But this, in a sense, is most characteristic of him. He didn't know who Johnny Sylvester was,

154

155

nor had he the faintest idea of what he had done for him. But whoever Johnny was and whatever he had done for him—he was glad of it.

If Johnny ever reads this, he shouldn't feel badly that the Babe didn't remember his name. He knew the names of some but not all of his teammates. Lou Gehrig, of course, and Herb Pennock and Bob Meusel and Waite Hoyt and Earle Combs and Tony Lazzeri and the rest of the regulars. The others? He had his own names for them. Jules Wera, a substitute infielder, was "Flop Ears." Garland Braxton, a pitcher, was "Chicken Neck." Myles Thomas, another pitcher, was "Duck Eye." A baseball writer assigned to the club had to be with it for at least a year before the Babe learned his name. Meanwhile, depending on his age, he was "Kid" or "Pop."

Once, as he dressed hurriedly after a game, and Pennock asked him why he was rushing, he said:

"I got a dinner date with . . . oh, you know. That movie actor and his wife that just got back from Europe."

"Douglas Fairbanks and Mary Pickford, by any chance?"

"Yeah," the Babe said. "That's them."

F. G.

Toward the end of the 1961 season Roger Maris invariably would have to face a horde of newsmen and photographers after each game. All of them, of course, were around him as a result of his assault on Babe Ruth's record and it became quite an ordeal for Maris.

Many of his teammates, seeing what he was going through with the press at his heels every day, openly sympathized with Maris.

"It's really rough on Maris, isn't it?" one writer said to

teammate Whitey Ford in the clubhouse after Rog hit his sixtieth homer.

"I don't sympathize with him," quipped Whitey, the team's jokester. "He brought it all on himself."

LEO PETERSON

Henry Aaron, listening to glowing words from Braves owner Lou Perini at a banquet several years ago, turned to then manager Charlie Grimm and asked, "Does he mean that after I sign or before I sign my contract?"

Aaron, during World Series against Yankees, stepped to the plate. Yogi Berra told him, "You've got the trademark in the wrong place. It should be in the front." To which Hank replied, "I get paid for hitting, not for reading."

Robin Roberts (on Hank Aaron): "He's the only hitter I know who can sleep between pitches."

RAY GRODY

Eddie Roush, who has his niche in the Hall of Fame at Cooperstown, and deservedly so, was born and reared in Oakland City, Indiana. Or, more properly, on a farm hard by Oakland City, which isn't exactly a metropolis. And how did he hit the trail that led him to the big leagues?

"The cows started me," he once said.

"The cows?"

"That's right. Winters can be *awful* cold in Indiana and winter mornings very dark. I used to have to get up at five o'clock to go out to the barn and milk the cows. I don't know whether or not the cows liked it but I didn't. I had to get away from them somehow. I was a pretty good ballplayer on the town team and I said to myself one dark and cold morning:

" 'That's for me.'

158

"I didn't think I'd ever get to the major leagues and in those days there wasn't any Hall of Fame, so I couldn't even dream of getting there. But I had to get rid of them cows."

F. G.

Minnie Minoso, veteran outfielder from Cuba, speaks Spanish almost all the time but when it is to his benefit he handles the English tongue even to the point of punning.

One day, while he was with the Chicago White Sox, a cute girl reporter invaded the Sox dugout at the start of the pregame warm-up to interview the slugger.

Minoso found it convenient to speak and understand English perfectly. Near the end of the session, Minoso suggested that she ask him whom he regarded as the best outfielder in the American League. The question, dutifully put, was answered with "Minoso."

"Are you sure?" asked the news-hen.

"Me-know-so," replied Minnie with a wink.

SPIKE CLAASSEN

Blondie Purcell was an outfielder with the Phillies in 1884, and following that season he found himself in a contract argument with his boss, Colonel John I. Rogers.

"If you do not pay me what I ask," he informed Rogers, "I will return to my former occupation."

"And what, may I ask, is that?" Rogers inquired.

Blondie looked at the floor. "Shoveling snow," he replied.

F. G.

Here is one about Charlie Maxwell that really happened:

Maxwell was sitting in the coffee shop of the Hotel Shoreham in Washington before a night game with the Senators.

He was having a light snack when I came in and sat next to him.

"I'll have a coffee milk shake," I said to the waitress.

"A coffee milk shake!" Maxwell boomed.

"Sure," I said. "I've got to have something to keep me awake when I watch you guys play."

Maxwell grinned. "Maybe so . . . but I'll bet more people have gone to sleep reading newspapers than watching ball games."

JOE FALLS

The moment which sticks with me most often is a gaunt, haggard DiMaggio sitting in the dressing room at Ebbets Field during the 1949 World Series.

He had missed half the year with his heel spur, come back to lead the Yanks to the pennant and hit only .111 in the series because of flu. But in that game he hit his only homer of the series.

His son (then about eight or nine as I recall) came up to Joe in the noise of the dressing room (I was sitting talking to Joe) and said: "Dad, I'm sorry but I lost that ball you gave me."

"That's all right, son," Joe said, ruffling the kid's hair and giving him a squeeze. "I lost one myself today."

OSCAR FRALEY

In the early 1930's, when the Washington Senators used to finish more respectably than in many, many seasons since, a violent and gifted young man named Alvin ("Jake") Powell came off the sandlots of the nation's capital. Jake could hit, run, field and throw, and the late Clark Griffith

160

set store not only by these skills but by the fact that Jake was a local boy.

Jake, who could perform his tasks on the ball field with an insolent ease, later was to take his own life with a pistol while being detained in a Washington police station. But in his younger days he was as exciting as Jim Piersall is today, and perhaps a better hitter.

After the Senators won the 1933 pennant (their last), Griffith decreed that Powell should inherit the center-field job from the steady but unspectacular Fred Schulte. But in training camp in Biloxi, Mississippi, Jake was known to absent himself at times and Joe Cronin, then manager-shortstop, fined him. Once, on the way north, Powell missed the train that was to stop at Cordele, Georgia, for an exhibition game.

Miraculously, it seemed, Powell was in uniform at game time. Bucky Harris, who had succeeded Cronin as the Senators' manager, was all set to fine him until his unexpected appearance. Later, under questioning, it developed that Jake had hired an airplane and put it on the Washington club's bill. Then he *did* draw a fine!

Old Griff, who played it rough and tumble himself in his pitching days, had a fondness for aggressive ballplayers. But Jake was a little too aggressive. He was ruthless on the bases and if he could get a crack at an infielder he would take him out. Once he seemingly ran into first baseman Hank Greenberg of the Tigers with a certain dedication and broke Hank's wrist, although Jake was a couple of steps later than the throw.

After one-third of the '36 season Griff decided that it would be more peaceful if he traded Powell. A Yankee-hater of long standing (Clark was the Yankees' first manager, although in those years of '03–'07 they were called the

Highlanders), the Old Fox nonetheless agreed to accept Ben Chapman, a fiery type himself, in exchange for Powell.

Griffith sensed the Yankees were going to win big in the future . . . as they did. (Four straight pennants, seven in eight years.) Still, he had to get rid of Powell and so Jake became the New York left fielder, with the rookie Joe Di-Maggio in center and George Selkirk in right.

The Yankees won, all right—by 19½ games. Right at the end of the '36 season the Senators were moving out of Chicago and the Yankees moving on. A Washington baseball writer shared a taxi with my friend Jake on the way from the Del Prado Hotel to Comiskey Park.

"How do you think you'll do against Hubbell?" the newspaperman asked Jake. The Giants were to play the Yankees in the World Series in a couple of days.

"Right or left?'" Powell murmured with no great show of interest.

"Hubbell!" repeated the other, incredulously. "He won 26 games. This is the best left-hander in the business. He throws a screwball that'll come up to a right-handed hitter like a great curve."

"You know," Jake replied, "I took them guys at the pinball machine last night. I dropped one in that 'Cha-nay' slot and picked it all up."

There was a hotel lobby pinball machine which the players fancied, a geographical-type gimmick in which a ball that nestled in "Detroit" might be worth 1,000 points, in "Memphis" 500, et cetera. Having been an investor in this machine, the writers pressed Jake for information as to how to win money by hitting "Cha-nay." "What part of the machine's map of North America does a guy look for this big deal?"

162

"Left side, high up," Jake confided. "It ain't spelled out too good, but I hit it." Research later revealed that Powell had won by inserting a steel ball into "Cheyenne, Wyoming."

"Look," the other stressed upon Jake in the taxi, "you're going to be in your first World Series. The Giants have pitchers: Hubbell . . . Fitzsimmons . . . Schumacher."

"Don't make no difference," Jake responded laconically. "I'll hit 'em."

And so he did. Hubbell beat the Yankees, 6–1, in the opener, but Powell raked him for a double and two singles in four times at bat. The Yanks made only seven hits in all.

The rampage by Jake continued. When the World Series was over, Yankees winning in six games, Powell, no less, was the top hitter with .455. He hit Schumacher and Fitz and Hubbell as he hit "Cha-nay" on the pinball machine.

FRANCIS STANN

When Arnold ("Jigger") Statz was managing Los Angeles, then in the Pacific Coast League, one of his outfielders was Louis Novikoff, who could murder minor league pitching (he didn't last long with the Cubs when he had his shot in the big show) but was, without meaning to be so, rather clownish on defense. Now the Angels were playing in Seattle and were leading by one run in the bottom half of the ninth, but Seattle got two men on base and, with two out, the hitter lined toward Louis. Louis came tearing in to make the putout that would end the game, stubbed his toe, and sprawled flat on his face. The ball went all the way to the fence, everybody scored, and the enemy had won again with the help of the hapless Novikoff.

As they trudged to the clubhouse, Jigger asked:

163

"What happened, Louis?"

And Novikoff blinked and asked, "When?"

F. G.

When Lefty O'Doul discovered that he'd never truly make the grade as a major league pitcher with the Yankees or the Red Sox after a four-year go at it and was back with San Francisco in the Pacific Coast League, he wisely switched to the outfield and, being a good hitter, shortly returned to the big show, this time with the Giants. He became a great hitter as he moved from the Giants to the Phillies, to the Dodgers and back to the Giants, but he was an erratic fielder: he would haul down fly balls or line drives that seemingly were out of his reach—then, like as not, drop one for which he'd scarcely had to move.

One day in 1934, his last year with the Giants, he found in his mail at the Polo Grounds a courteous note from a saloonkeeper in the Times Square area which read as follows:

"I am enclosing your check for ten dollars that I cashed for you the other night. As you can see, the bank rejected it for the reason that you have no account there. I am sure there must be a mistake and also sure that you will rectify it."

It was, of course, a forgery. After the game, Lefty went downtown, found the saloon, and asked for the proprietor.

"Did you ever see me before?" he asked.

"No," the man said, "why?"

"I'm Lefty O'Doul. Here's my San Francisco driver's license to prove it."

Naturally, the man was embarrassed and apologized, and Lefty said:

"Look, I have a place of my own in San Francisco and I've had bum checks put over on me, too."

164

LIFE ON THE FARM

He dropped a $20 bill on the bar and said:

"That's to cover your loss and buy a round for these gentlemen," nodding toward four or five customers. "Now, let me give you a tip: when that guy came in here and said he was Lefty O'Doul, you should have taken him out in the backyard and hit a fungo to him. If he caught it, you would know he was a phony."

F. G.

In 1953 Lawton Carver, then sports editor of International News Service, made an arrangement with Mickey Mantle to "cover" the World Series for INS, and I was assigned to operate the Mick's typewriter.

Mantle has acquired considerably more *savoir-faire* through the years, I understand, but in '53 he was still a youngster, very reticent and very moody. As it turned out, he was like the little girl with the curl in that series—either very, very good or horrid.

On days when he had been heroic his comments were monosyllabic. On the bad days (primarily involving several strikeouts) it was worse; he sat in front of his locker with his head in his hands and said nothing at all. If there is such a thing as poetic license, then you could say that Mantle's ghost really had to use his haunting license to fill the allotted space. In short, ghosting was ghastly until the final game.

Now, this was the series in which Billy Martin came down to the wire needing one hit for a record, and Mantle and Martin, as you know, were very close pals. On his last at bat, Billy's infield smash was ruled an error by the scorers, and he missed his chance for a record.

Back in the locker room (the Yanks had won this series, by the way), Mantle looked me in the eye for the first time since the opening game.

"This is supposed to be my story?" he asked. "I can say anything I want?"

With visions of a real beat, I assured him it was so and waited, my pencil at the ready.

"Well, I just want to say that whoever the blankety-blank scorer was made that call on Martin is a blind blankety-blank-blank-blank," he said.

No doubt I looked nonplused, and several other players who were standing around guffawed.

"No, I guess you couldn't print that," said Mickey. His brow furrowed in thought for a minute, and then this shy, inarticulate kid drew himself up and said with a flourish and, I thought, real pride of authorship:

"Okay, just say it was rank injustice."

JOHN BARRINGTON

Sam Rice was a Washington outfielder when Bucky Harris managed the Senators.

Rice played the same field as Babe Ruth and during a game with the Yankees, after booting a ground ball he complained when the inning was over as he came to the bench: "That damned Ruth."

"What the hell did Ruth have to do with you booting that ball?"

"The ——— spits so much tobacco juice around out there that you can hardly stand up much less field a grounder."

LAWTON CARVER

168

VII. Umpires

Charles Taylor, an umpire in the International Association of 1878, was the only "man in blue" known to have inserted an advertisement in the newspapers to justify his decisions.

Apparently infuriated by criticism of his work in Utica, New York, Taylor signed the following advertisement in the Utica *Observer:*

Complaint has been made as to the calling of strikes and balls. If the directors and scorers were about 12 feet lower, they would be better able to criticize my decisions. I will admit they can plainly see when a ball passes over the plate, but they should also admit in return that I am better able to judge with accuracy the fairness of a high or low ball. When the ball passes over the plate, my head is on a level with the striker's waist, while the heads of those in the scorer's stand are at least 12 to 14 feet above the plate. There may be other questionable decisions, as one of my critics chooses to call them, but as these (balls and strikes) are the ones being questioned, these are the ones on which I offer explanation. It has been remarked that when the Utica club wins, the umpire is all that could be asked. When they lose, one doubtful decision by that unfortunate official, which may or may not be an error, throws all the blame on his shoulders, *undoubted* errors by the players having nothing whatsoever to do with the result.

JOSEPH M. OVERFIELD

Red Jones, former American League umpire, was behind the plate at Yankee Stadium one day with Tommy Byrne, a wild southpaw, on the mound for the home team opposing the Detroit Tigers.

Byrne was even wilder than usual this day and once he threw six straight balls, all of them low and outside. With every pitch, Yogi Berra would pull the ball back into the strike zone. But the trick didn't fool Jones. Berra, without turning around, protested every call but kept his protests on an informal basis by not turning around to address the umpire directly.

Byrne finally got the side out and who should stride to the plate as a batter to open the Yankee half of the inning but Berra!

The first ball pitched to him by the Tiger moundsman was low and outside—approximately the very same spot which Byrne had been finding so consistently.

"Steeeerike," yelled Jones.

Berra spun around, jumped out of the box and screamed, "That was a ball, Red, it was just like those Byrne threw."

"You are right," replied Jones, "that is what I kept telling you when Byrne was throwing."

SPIKE CLAASSEN

Bill McGowan, American League umpire, was having a ham sandwich and a cup of coffee in the Stevens commissary at the Yankee Stadium an hour or so before game time on a Tuesday when Mark Roth, the Yanks' road secretary, came by.

"A fine Mick you are," Mark said, "eating a ham sandwich on Friday."

Bill almost choked.

"What day is this?" he asked, in sudden panic.

"That's a hot one," Mark said, still walking. "Here's a guy going to umpire a ball game and he don't even know what day it is."

F. G.

One of my favorite sports characters during more than half a century of sports writing, was the late William J. ("Bill") Guthrie who umpired in the American and National Leagues along with officiating in the three Triple A minor leagues—American Association, International and Pacific Coast Leagues. His umpiring career covered a period of forty-one years before he died a decade or so ago.

I first became acquainted with Guthrie when he was umpiring in the American Association in 1909. "Bull-Necked Bill," as baseball managers and players referred to the burly arbiter, was one of the most colorful umpires in baseball annals. In this respect he ranked with Bill Klem, Tim Hurst, Silk O'Loughlin, Hank O'Day, George Moriarty, Jack Sheridan, Bill Dinneen, Billy Evans, and "Beans" Reardon.

When I reminded Bill during an interview years ago that he never had any serious trouble with managers and players during his lengthy career, he said in his slangy "dese-dem-dat-dose" manner:

"Dat's right, Barton. I call 'em quick and den I walk away wid my arms bow-legged, tough like, ya know. If the managers and players follow me, beefing, I tell 'em dat's da way

I sees it. I ask 'em if dey wants to quit arguin', or take a shower."

Strange as it may seem, during his lengthy career as an umpire Guthrie was popular with managers and players alike because, in addition to being a top-notch umpire, he never carried grudges off the field. Heated arguments were forgotten by game time the next day.

The story has been told that Ban Johnson, when president of the American League, dismissed Guthrie upon the insistence of Miller Huggins, manager of the Yankees, and the top brass of the Yanks, for calling Huggins a bat boy.

"That yarn was a lot of hooey," Guthrie told me when I asked him about it. "Little Hug and I was the best of friends. Johnson fired me because I refused to serve as a stoolpigeon for him on certain club owners, managers, and players in the American League.

"Getting back to Hug and me, here's what really happened:

"The Yankees are playing Washington in Washington and I called out Babe Ruth on strikes. The big fellow called me some names I didn't like, so I give him the bum's rush to the clubhouse. Hug took up the argument and gave me a bad time, so I have to run him outa da game, too.

" 'Hey, Babe,' I yelled. He was almost to the runway leading to de Yanks' clubhouse under the stands by this time, so I had to yell good and loud. When Babe turned around, I pointed to Huggins and says: 'Take da bat boy wit ya.'

"Several days later I'm standing near Huggins in the Yankees' dugout in New York. It's raining and I'm punching the bag with Hug.

" 'Listen, Bill,' Hug says, 'you can give me a blast and shoo me out of a game if I get out of line, but don't ever call me a bat boy again. Nothing ever made me so mad as that

172

crack. When I came home after the Washington series, my sister, who keeps house for me in New York, wanted to know what I did to be put out of the game. When I told her what you said, she laughed and laughed. That made me madder than ever. But Sis got such a kick out of it that I finally laughed with her. Nevertheless, I still don't think it's funny. No more of that bat boy stuff, understand?' "

" 'Okay, Hug,' I says, 'from now on during games I'll call you Mr. Huggins and you call me Mr. Guthrie.' That's how it was between Hug and me during the rest of the season. The little guy and me was the best of friends up to the time he died. Hug was one of the nicest fellows I ever knew in baseball. I might add, Barton, he was a great manager and knew how to handle men."

Guthrie was still umpiring in the American Association when Ted Williams played with the Minneapolis Millers in 1938, and your reporter was covering the Minneapolis team.

The Millers opened the season at Louisville. Guthrie was umpiring behind the plate.

The first time Williams came to bat, Guthrie called him out on strikes.

Ted, then only 19 years old, lost his temper; kicked dirt around the plate and then hurled his bat high into the air to show his disgust at Guthrie's decision.

Bill removed his mask, looked up in the air, and said: "Well, kid, if dat bat comes down, you're outa da game."

GEORGE A. BARTON

Albert ("Dolly") Stark was one of the best umpires the major leagues ever have known, yet, having entered the National League in 1928, he retired in 1940 although still a young man. When asked why he had stepped down at the very peak of his brilliant career, he pulled no punches in his reply.

"I just got sick and tired of it," he said. "Umpiring behind the plate, you might make a couple of hundred decisions in a day's work. On the bases, you're straining to be on top of every play and in exactly the right spot to see the play and call it. Every decision is important. There is no such thing as a casual or unimportant decision in a ball game. And you've always got to be right.

"You match your wits with all the great minds of the game. They called McGraw the Little Napoleon because he was such a great strategist. Every manager is a mastermind. They're all so smart and you've got to be smarter so you're not outsmarted. You know the rules better than they do, you know every aspect of the game, so you can always be ready for the play.

"So what happens? You're abused, taunted and ridiculed. Incompetents who aren't good enough to play every day sit on the bench and enjoy themselves calling you the vilest names imaginable. The responsibility for the honest and decent conduct of baseball is laid in your lap every afternoon and if you expect to be adequately paid for your responsibility and ability they look at you as if you had called them a dirty name.

"It isn't that I couldn't take this sort of thing any more. I wouldn't take it."

F. G.

All umpires take themselves seriously but a few, such as Bill Byron, managed to squeeze some fun out of their difficult assignments. Bill, who served in the National League from 1913 through 1919, was known as "Lord Byron, the Singing Umpire," for in his retorts to managers or players

174

THIS COULD BE
ANOTHER CLASSIC!

175

critical of his judgment he frequently would set his words to music or couch them in rhyme of a sort.

When, for instance, he called Casey Stengel, then an outfielder with the Dodgers, out in a close play at the plate in a game with the Giants at the Polo Grounds and then chased him for having protested too long and too profanely, he hummed to the still raging player:

> To the clubhouse you must go
> You must go
> You must go
> To the clubhouse you must go
> My fair Casey.

Admonishing hitters who violently disagreed with him when he called them out on strikes, he would taunt them with:

> Let me tell you something, son,
> Before you get much older,
> You cannot hit the ball, my friend,
> With your bat upon your shoulder.

F. G.

Barry McCormick was the umpire back of the plate in Boston on May 1, 1920, when the Braves and the Dodgers set a major league endurance record and it was he who called the game in the gathering gloom at the end of the twenty-sixth inning with the starting pitchers, Joe Oeschger for the Braves and Leon Cadore for the Dodgers, still in action.

Ivan Olson, the Brooklyn shortstop—and a sturdy man he was—lodged the lone protest.

"Give us one more inning!" he yelled.

177

"Why?" Barry asked.

"So we can say we played three full games in one afternoon," Olson said.

"Not without miners' lamps on your caps," Barry countered, and walked off the field.

F. G.

Clarence Owens, called "Brick" because he was built as solidly as a brick smokehouse, had a spirit as rugged as his body. No one ever awed him and by his manner he offered no encouragement to those who would bait him.

"Call 'em loud and walk away tough" was his advice to young aspirants to the trade. Yet once this proud soul humbled himself before his boss in the time before his elevation to the majors. The story was told by Joseph D. O'Brien, then president of the American Association:

"In an important series in Milwaukee Brick enraged the crowd with a decision on a close play at the plate. As a safety measure—and over his bitter protests—the police guarded him as he left the field after the game and some really vicious fans threatened that if he returned the next day they would maim him. I was in Chicago when I heard of this and took the next train up to Milwaukee and called Brick to my room at the hotel.

" 'I don't usually take these things seriously,' I told him, 'but this time I do. For your own good, I am going to pull you off this series.'

"You would have thought I had struck him in the face.

" 'No! No!' he cried. 'Don't do that to me, Mr. O'Brien!'

"I insisted that I would and suddenly he threw himself on his knees before me, tears in his eyes.

" 'Please,' he said softly. 'Please, Mr. O'Brien!'

"I never was so moved by anything as by the sight of this

178

brave man pleading for his right to face an angry mob on a field where he would be an open target for bottles or other missiles thrown from the stand. I was pretty close to tears myself as I said:

"'All right, Brick. I'm not going to replace you.'

"Fortunately, nothing happened the next day. He was hooted and otherwise verbally abused, of course, when he swaggered onto the field but his courage earned for him the grudging respect of the hooligans who, I am convinced, really had meant to do him bodily harm."

F. G.

Not all the famous umpires achieved their fame in the major leagues. In his fine book *The Umpire Story*, James M. Kahn wrote:

The most celebrated of these minor league veterans was Harry Samuel ("Steamboat") Johnson, who died in 1950 after forty years of umpiring, the last thirty of them in the Southern League. Steamboat's career was a riotous one, frequently marked with violence on the giving as well as on the receiving end, because "The Steamer," as Southern League fans got to call him, was fearless and not above getting in the first swipe himself if an assailant looked as though he was getting ready to let one go. In his own story of his life which he published in 1935 under the title *Standing the Gaff*, he included a few vital statistics:

"I have rendered about one million decisions since I began umpiring in 1909. Something like four thousand bottles have been thrown at me in my day but only about twenty ever hit me. That does not speak very well for the accuracy of the fans' throwing."

No one intimidated Steamboat and he was no more awed

by the great names of baseball than he was by the obscure ones. In the spring of 1923 Ty Cobb, then managing Detroit, hired Johnson to umpire a ten-game exhibition series which the Tigers were to play with the St. Louis Cardinals in Augusta, Georgia. It was a series that had attracted tremendous interest throughout Georgia, with Cobb, its great native son, the champion batter of the American League, matched with Rogers Hornsby, the bright St. Louis star who was the champion batsman of the National League. Fans poured into Augusta from miles around and jammed the ball park for the opening game. It was hardly the ideal setting in which to forfeit a ball game but that's precisely what Steamboat did in the sixth inning, when Cobb became embroiled in an argument with Cy Pfirman, the National League umpire and Johnson's partner. Cobb was ordered out of the game but refused to go. Instead, he went to his position in center field.

Pfirman came over to Johnson and told him he had put Cobb out of the game and that the Detroit manager would have to leave before the game went on. Johnson strolled out to center field and told Cobb he would have to leave but Ty refused.

"I told Cobb that I was in a terrible position," Johnson said, "because I knew that if I forfeited the game he would fire me and I would lose out on the exhibition series. Cobb told me I was exactly right; that he would fire me if I forfeited the game.

"I then told Cobb that if he had not left the game by the time I returned to home plate I would forfeit the game to St. Louis. Ty warned me that if I forfeited the game the fans would mob me. I told him I would just as soon be killed on a ball field as anywhere else."

Upon reaching the plate, Johnson turned and saw that

180

Cobb was still in center field, and so, removing his cap, and bellowing in the foghorn voice which had earned him his nickname, Johnson announced to the jammed stands that he was forfeiting the game to St. Louis because Cobb would not leave the field.

Neither Johnson nor Pfirman was assaulted as they walked across the field to their dressing room. They were pushed and jostled and all the buttons were torn off Pfirman's uniform coat but they were otherwise unharmed. The admission money had to be refunded and Cobb came tearing into the umpires' dressing room to tell Johnson what he thought of him and to make good on his threat to fire him. Steamboat was very definitely on the spot but later that evening as he was packing his things at his hotel to go back to his home in Memphis, Johnson got a phone call from Cobb, telling him that the rumpus was all over and that he should come back to finish out his contract, which he did.

It was of such scuffles, and more, year after year, that Steamboat's life story is comprised but his honesty, courage and simplicity and the humor he usually brought to bear on even the most desperate situations, in time earned him a unique place among minor league umpires. He was not only regarded with esteem but actually was held in affection and became a Southern League hero and favorite, as well as a Southern League institution.

"Steamboat Johnson is as full of color as a circus parade," Ed Danforth, sports editor of the *Atlanta Georgian,* wrote of him. "He is one umpire who is a standout. He is a real attraction. Fans often come to the park just to see him work."

Johnson had one year in the National League—in 1914. At the end of the season his contract was not renewed. He was puzzled by it, never understood it, was a little bit

181

hurt by it, and never quite got over it. It was an old and painful wound to his pride. But once he settled down in the Southern League and reconciled himself to a career of minor league umpiring, he brought to it a quality of humor, personal authority and rugged individualism which was every bit as distinctive as that of Bill Klem in the National League.

Steamboat was proud of his voice and would announce the batteries before the game in coarse, vibrant syllables that quivered the rafters of the Southern League ball parks. He scorned the mechanical amplifiers and is reported to have brooded for quite some time after they eventually replaced the natural lung power of the umpires. He was likewise affirmative about his eyesight and would have his eyes examined regularly by an oculist and get a certificate attesting to their sharpness. He carried this in his uniform pocket and when a batter questioned his eyesight or he was otherwise referred to as a "blind robber," he would produce it.

"Read this, young man," he would say. "Twenty-twenty in each eye."

Steamboat lived in Memphis where, with his wife, he ran a restaurant, "Steamboat Johnson's Eat Shoppe," a favorite place for cotton men. He was a popular and respected figure in his home town and finally, in 1949, when he was rounding out his thirtieth year in the Southern League, was paid an extraordinary compliment by Southern League fans when, on July 28 in New Orleans, they held a "night" for him.

In keeping with Johnson's most colorful performances and character, he made his appearance on the ball field to receive the homage of the fans, manacled to a policeman, wearing dark blue glasses and led by a seeing-eye dog, a mite of a smooth-haired fox terrier. Three other Southern League umpires were present for the occasion and, to comprise part of the honors which were to go to Steamboat on his night, were permitted to reverse the usual procedure and boo the fans, which they did with enthusiasm and gusto. It remains a tribute to an umpire, hilarious as it was, unparalleled in minor league history, a unique climax to a unique career.

Frank Frisch and "Beans" Reardon, the umpire, were very good friends but this did not prevent them from having many a lively row on the field. When Frisch was managing the Cardinals, he and his coach, Mike Gonzalez, shared a suite in the Hotel Coronado when the club was at home and Beans also put up there when he was assigned to St. Louis. And after the game every day, Frank and Mike and Beans would meet in the bar for a few beers and some iced shrimp before dinner.

One day, late in the game, Frank and Beans got into a frightful row and when Beans ordered Frank to leave the field he refused to do so at first and yielded, after a delay of five minutes or more, only when Beans threatened to forfeit the game. Back at the hotel an hour or so later, Frank and Mike were in the bar but there was no sign of Beans.

"Where do you suppose he is?" Frank asked.

"I don't know," Mike said. "Call his room."

Frank did and Beans answered.

"What are you doing up there?" Frank snapped. "Waiting for the beer to get warm?"

"I'll tell you what I'm doing!" Beans said. "I'm writing a report that I'm going to wire Ford Frick" (then president of the National League) "about what happened today and recommend that he suspend you!"

"Go ahead!" Frank yelled. "Get the ———— thing off and come down here! We're not going to wait all night for you!"

A short time later Beans appeared in the bar.

"I took good care of you, you Dutch ———," he said.

They were drinking their beer and eating their shrimp when Beans asked:

"Are you using your car tonight?"

"No," Frank said.

"Then call the garage and tell the man to bring it around. There's a friend of mine from San Francisco in town and I want to take him to dinner."

"Why, you———!" Frank said, reaching for the telephone.

"And while you're at it," Beans said, "tell him to fill it up. I may go far and stay late."

Before game time the next day, Frank received a wire from Ford Frick:

"Effective immediately, you are suspended for five days, as recommended by umpire Reardon because of your conduct on the field yesterday."

F. G.

There never was a more dedicated umpire than Bill Klem, who once, dramatically and truly, shouted:

"Baseball is more to me than the greatest game in the world! It is a religion!"

Convinced that he never made a mistake in his life, he said simply:

"If it was a ball, why did I call it a strike? If a man was safe, why did I call him out? I call a strike, a ball, or a play the way I see it—and the way I see it is the way it was."

A supreme egotist? Of course. A man must be an egotist to become an umpire. Klem was the greatest umpire because, apart from his other qualifications, he had the greatest ego.

No one ever awed him—players, managers, owners, league presidents or the stern, often harsh Kenesaw Mountain Landis, baseball's first commissioner, who had a savage contempt for the owners he often smote with an iron fist. Bill had his brush with Landis over horse race betting—which also was a kind of religion with him, but on which Landis frowned, purely as a matter of policy fashioned when he discovered too many ballplayers were becoming involved with bookmakers. He summoned Bill to his office in Chicago and his opening question was:

"William, is it true that you bet on the horses?"

The question, couched in friendly words and manner mild though it was, pulled Bill out of his chair:

"I do, Commissioner!" he thundered. *And pay off one hundred cents on the dollar!"*

There were no more questions, no reproofs, no warnings. Bill strode from the room a free man, free to continue to play the horses—which he did virtually to the day he died.

His principal antagonist throughout his big league career was John McGraw. The struggle between them began in 1905, when they first met on the field, and endured until McGraw's retirement in 1932, with major engagements frequently taking place. After the first, in which Bill ordered the Giant manager from the game, McGraw snarled:

"I'm going to get your job, you busher!"

And Bill said: "Mr. Manager, if it's possible for you to get my job away from me, I don't want it."

Bill's battle cry in this ceaseless warfare was:

"I'll stop McGraw or McGraw will stop me!"

Neither succeeded in stopping the other. John simply wore out before Bill did. Meanwhile, as in the case of Frisch and Reardon, they were frequent companions off the field, dining, drinking, playing bridge, or going to the races. But their friendship was put in cold storage whenever the Giants went into action with Klem back of the plate or on the bases.

A year before Bill's death in 1951, he wrote in his autobiography, published in *Collier's*:

"John J. McGraw left behind him millions of admirers. He left none who fought him as often as I did and he left none who had as many pleasant hours with him as I did. John McGraw *off* the field was a man in every old-fashioned sense of the word. He helped his friends; he fought for his rightful due with words, fists or whatever came readily to hand; his charity knew neither restraint nor publicity.

"But John McGraw *on* the field was a detriment to baseball until he resigned as the Giants' manager."

F. G.

Back in the twenties, Bill McGowan and Roy Van Graflan worked as a team and, to perfect their gestures, would practice before a mirror in their hotel room.

"Out!" Bill would yell, jerking a thumb over his shoulder, then holding the pose while studying it in the glass.

"Out!" Roy would bellow, making a motion of his own devising.

They would take time out to criticize each other's gyrations. Then:

"Out!" would be the cry again.

One night their telephone rang. McGowan answered it and a voice said:

"I'm the man in the next room. I don't mind the noise you're making but tell me: Don't you guys ever call a runner safe?"

F. G.

VIII. Scouts

One of John McGraw's assets as manager of the New York Giants was his private, unofficial scouting force made up of his friends—old ballplayers, college coaches, minor league club owners and managers, former umpires, and just plain fans with a knowledge of true baseball values. Frank Frisch, for instance, was sent to him by Arthur Devlin, third baseman on his first pennant-winning team (1904), who became the coach at Fordham University, and Hal Schumacher by a man in upstate New York who had known him from the time he was playing in towns such as Wellsville and Olean.

One of the most notable examples of the functioning of this far-flung corps occurred on a rainy day in Memphis in the spring of 1922 when the Giants were en route from their training camp at San Antonio to New York. Among his callers in his suite at the Hotel Peabody were Kid Elberfeld, an old companion and sparring partner from the baseball trails in the nineties, who then was the manager in Little Rock, and Tom Watkins, who owned the Memphis club.

Separately, but only an hour or so apart, as they sat with John over a jug of the best bootleg liquor that could be bought in the whole state of Tennessee at the time, they gave him leads to ballplayers destined to achieve fame at the Polo Grounds.

"I got a shortstop for you, Mac," Elberfeld said. "Comes from right over here in Waldo, Arkansas. Have somebody watch him and if he has a good year, buy him."

"There's a boy in this town who has been pitching in this league for three or four years and he's one of the best hitters in the league, too," Watkins said. "But he wanted to stay home, so he quit and got a job with the Standard Oil Company and plays with their team, the Polarines, on Saturdays and Sundays. I'll ask him to come up and see you and you can talk to him. I think he might be willing to leave home for a chance to make it in the big leagues."

The shortstop was Travis Jackson. The pitcher, whom McGraw switched from the box to first base, was Bill Terry.

F. G.

Dick Kinsella, out of Springfield, Illinois, was a Giant scout and turned up many a ballplayer for John McGraw, among them Larry Doyle, who not only became famous as a hard-hitting second baseman but always will be remembered as the one who said, in his early days at the Polo Grounds:

"It's great to be young and a Giant."

Dick could have been, on his appearance, a retired "heavy" in melodramas—fairly tall, solidly built, with classic features topped by thick jet-black hair and eyebrows to match. Actually, he was a paint store proprietor, a thoroughly qualified judge of ballplayers and a friend of McGraw's from the nineties, when John played with Cedar Rapids. He also was interested in politics and, in 1928, was a delegate to the Democratic National Convention in Houston that was to nominate Al Smith for the Presidency.

188

On a dull day at the convention, when he knew nothing of importance could happen, Dick's mind turned, naturally, to baseball and he decided to go to the Texas League ball game, with Beaumont as the visiting club. He didn't go for professional reasons. He just wanted an afternoon in the sunshine, as a spectator at his favorite sport. But that afternoon he saw Carl Hubbell pitching for Beaumont.

He'd never seen Hubbell before but he knew of him. Carl had been up with the Detroit club twice. The first time, Ty Cobb was the manager. The second time around, George Moriarty sat in judgment on him. Each was convinced that the screwball, which was his most effective pitch, would ruin his arm. Now he was on the Tigers' farm club in Beaumont, his potentially great talent for sale, as Dick learned. So Dick forsook the convention and followed Hubbell around the Texas League circuit and when he was convinced that what he'd seen at Houston was not a mirage he called McGraw and said:

"Buy this young man, John. He has it. You know what Cobb and Moriarty said about him but . . ."

"I know," McGraw said. "The screwball would ruin his arm. Matty had a screwball, too, only in those days they called it the fadeaway . . . and it didn't ruin his arm. Find out what they want for him and I'll have the check in the mail as soon as I hear from you. I want him for instant delivery."

There was another call from Kinsella to McGraw. The check was put in the mail. Hubbell was on his way.

F. G.

It has only been in recent years that the major league clubs have assembled scouting staffs. In the piping times

189

before baseball became big business one scout, or two at most, seemed adequate.

In 1911 the Dodgers' scout was Larry Sutton. He was a tall, broad-shouldered, solemn-looking man, who wore steel-rimmed glasses and a derby hat and, rain or shine, carried an umbrella. He had been a printer but he knew baseball and he knew a major leaguer when he saw one in the raw and had so impressed Charles H. Ebbets by recommending some good players to him that Ebbets took him out of the print shop and put him on the Brooklyn payroll. His territory was limited only by his imagination and his budget for traveling expenses—which was smaller than his imagination by far, because in those days Ebbets was having a difficult time building a ball club and knocking down his debts.

This day in 1911 Larry was in Chicago and at a loose end, wanting to go somewhere but not knowing where to go. Later he told Ebbets:

"I walked into a railroad station and saw there was a train going to Aurora. I'd never been to Aurora but I knew they had a ball club there in some small league but I didn't know what it was. So I went there and saw this fellow playing in the outfield and, right off, I liked him. He was a good hitter and could throw, and what I liked best about him was that he was a hustler."

The fellow was on the Aurora club of the Wisconsin-Illinois League. His name was Casey Stengel.

F. G.

Tom Greenwade, scouting for the Yankees, found Mickey Mantle, seventeen years old, playing for the high school team in Commerce, Oklahoma. Later Tom was to say:

190

"I knew then how Paul Krichell must have felt the first time he saw Lou Gehrig."

The first time Krichell saw Gehrig was in the early spring of 1923, when he was waiting for the minor leagues to get under full headway and, meanwhile, was dropping in on college games in the vicinity of New York. One of these games was between Columbia and Rutgers at New Brunswick, New Jersey, where his attention was caught by a broad-shouldered, piano-legged youth who played in the Columbia outfield and hit the ball with terrific force. Returning to New York on the train with the Columbia team, he asked Andy Coakley, the coach, about the boy. Andy said:

"He's one of my pitchers but when he's not pitching I play him in the outfield because of his hitting. Come up to Baker Field next Tuesday. I'm going to pitch him against Penn and I think you might like him."

That night Paul called Ed Barrow, then general manager of the Yankees, and said:

"Don't laugh, but I think I saw another Ruth today. He played in the outfield but he's a pitcher and I'm going to see him pitch against Penn next Tuesday and I'll find out if he can hit all the time like he did today."

After the Penn game Paul, now really excited, called Barrow again.

"He hit a ball out of Baker Field and across 116th Street and it landed on the steps of the library!" he yelled into the phone. "I never saw anybody but Ruth who could hit a ball like that!"

Barrow, who had a tremendous respect for Paul's judgment, asked:

"Do you think we can get him?"

193

"He and Coakley will be at the office tomorrow morning," Paul said.

F. G.

Residing quietly in retirement in St. Paul, Minnesota, is Robert J. ("Bob") Connery, one of the major leagues' most successful baseball scouts.

Connery, now 81, is enjoying unusually fine health for a man of his years. He is amazingly alert and continues to maintain keen interest in baseball and national and international affairs. Never having married, Bob resides at the exclusive St. Paul Athletic Club where he enjoys the friendship of a legion of men among the elite of St. Paul's professional and business men.

Since retiring from baseball as owner of the St. Paul club of the American Association in 1935, Connery has done right well financially dabbling in stocks and bonds.

Prior to buying the St. Paul club in 1925, Connery, first as scout for the St. Louis Cardinals during the years his close friend, Miller Huggins, managed the Red Birds; and later with the Yankees after Huggins assumed management of the Yankees, Connery established an enviable reputation for discovering and signing young players who became major league stars.

One of the greatest highlights in Connery's scouting career was discovering and signing Rogers Hornsby for the Cardinals for $700.

Hornsby is still regarded as the greatest right-handed hitter in baseball annals, along with being a corking good second baseman and a brilliant manager and strategist.

I will let Bob Connery tell you in his own words how he found Hornsby playing in a small league, and then, with the aid of the late Miller Huggins, helped to develop Hornsby into the great player that he became.

"In 1914, the second year I scouted for the Cardinals," said Connery, "Miller Huggins, then manager of the Cards, split his squad for a series of spring exhibition games.

"Miller had me take one team to Dennison, Texas, which had a club in the Texas-Oklahoma League. We played a three-game series.

"Dennison had a gangling kid, 17 years old, playing second base, who caught my eye in the first game. The more I looked at that kid the more I liked him. He was green and awkward, but he possessed a great pair of hands. He fielded bad hoppers with exceptional skill, and got the ball away fast and accurately in plays at first and second base.

"I could tell by his every move that the kid did everything instinctively and easily. Moreover, you could tell he loved to play baseball. He showed a lot of hustle in the field and handled himself at the plate like a natural hitter.

"I used four good pitchers during the series—Slim Sallee, Red Ames, Bill Doakes and Bob Harmon. They already had established reputations in the National League. But they didn't scare that kid one whit. He crowded the plate, seldom offered at bad pitches, and came up with a hit or two in each of the three games.

"The boy's name was Rogers Hornsby.

"After the first game, I called the boy over to me and said: 'You like to play baseball, don't you, son?'

" 'I sure do, mister,' the kid replied. 'I want to be a big-leaguer some day.' "

"Young Hornsby looked so good that after I returned to San Antonio where the Cardinals were training, I told Huggins I had seen a fine prospect at Dennison and would like to go back and watch the boy some more.

195

"Back I went to Dennison. First thing I noticed was young Hornsby had a cheap glove and cheap shoes. A good ball-player, like a good workman, must have good tools, so I bought young Hornsby the best quality glove and shoes.

"My interest in the boy perked him up immensely and he made some plays around second base that convinced me all the more he was gifted with heaps of natural talent. I didn't like the way he batted, however. He was what we call a 'choke hitter.' Hornsby gripped his bat almost in the middle and poked at the ball. I knew that was a fault that could be easily overcome.

"After watching young Hornsby for a couple of weeks and being more and more impressed with his all-around ability, I bought him from the owner of the Dennison club for $700. The Dennison club owner thought he had made a great deal.

"Hornsby got his big chance early in 1915 when Roy Corhan, regular shortstop for the Cardinals, hurt his right arm. Huggins sent Rogers to short. The youngster made good from the outset. His fielding was brilliant and he played such smart heads-up baseball that he took Corhan's job away from him.

"Huggins and I changed Hornsby's batting style. We had him grip the bat at the end and take a full, natural swing and follow through, instead of gripping the bat near the middle and poking at the ball.

"It's a good thing young Hornsby possessed plenty of courage and determination, otherwise he would have become discouraged and given up. He struck out frequently and tapped easy flies and grounders to the infielders. But, instead of being discouraged, the youngster showed he had the right stuff in him by bearing down all the harder. The boy was so eager to improve his hitting that he persuaded

me to pitch to him mornings and late in the afternoon after
ball games. He shagged the balls after hitting them. All I
had to do was throw and give advice.

"There was no keeping down a lad with Hornsby's natural
ability and ambition. In due time he mastered the knack of
hitting the way Huggins and I wanted him to hit.

"The rest is history. Hornsby became the greatest right-
handed batter of all time, and one of the finest second basemen. He also developed into one of the outstanding managers in the major leagues. He richly deserved the success he
achieved because no ballplayer worked harder than Rogers
did to improve himself in every department of the game."

GEORGE A. BARTON

IX. Managers

Marse Joe McCarthy's
Do-and-Don't List

Joe McCarthy once listed all these proverbs for baseball:
Don't throw the ball before you catch it.

Take the bat off your shoulder if you want to become a .300 hitter.

Outfielders who throw the ball behind a runner lock the barn after the horse is stolen.

Keep your head up and you may not have to hold it down.

When you start to slide, slide. He who changes his mind may change a good leg for a broken leg.

Don't alibi on the bad hops. Anybody can stop the good ones.

Look ahead, not backwards, on the bases. Remember what happened to Lot's wife.

Don't throw the ball to the base after the runner is there. A ball in the hand is safer than the one in the air.

Touch all the bases. That's what they're there for.

Don't find too many faults with the umpire. You can't expect him to be as perfect as you are.

Nobody ever became a good ballplayer by walking after a ball.

Don't quit; the game is never over until the last man is out.

A pitcher hasn't anything if he hasn't control.

LES BIEDERMAN

Eddie Glennon was formerly the business manager of the Birmingham club of the Southern Association. In his travels around the country during the off-season Glennon found that the first question people asked was almost always the same one. So, he had cards printed which read quite simply: "I finished second. How did you do in your business?"

F. G.

The baseball season is approaching and pretty soon the umpire will throw out the first manager.

D. H.

Paul Waner had been drinking well if not wisely and grabbed an onion at the concession stand to kill booze fumes for the clubhouse meeting called by manager George Gibson. Gibson's sensitive nose crinkled at the onion smell but Paul explained he was partial to onions because it helped his power. Waner got four for four that afternoon and Gibson was urging his players to sample onions. "They'll give you power, looka Paul," he counseled.

MAX KASE

One year Casey Stengel came out of the dugout to yank a pitcher who was being clobbered. The pitcher pleaded to stay in, then demanded: "Why do I have to go out?" Casey pointed to the stands and softly replied:

"Up there people are beginning to talk."

F. G.

Joe Engel once tried to sign a rookie for his Chattanooga club of the Southern Association. "Double the salary or count me out," the rookie wrote. So Engel wired in return: "1-2-3-4-5-6-7-8-9-10."

F. G.

One winter after Paul Waner had had one of his finest seasons he got his contract in the mails at Ada, Oklahoma, calling for the same pay he had received the previous year.

Paul was scorched. There were no planes in those days, so Waner hopped the first rattler to Pittsburgh to see old man Dreyfuss (Barney) the owner.

He stormed into the office at Forbes Field and said:

"What's the meaning of this, Mr. Dreyfuss? There must be some mistake. I led the league in hitting, hit the most doubles, the most triples, had the most RBIs, and scored the most runs in the league last year. I don't get a raise for all this?"

As you may recall, Barney was a great man to keep up to date on statistics.

He pulled the stats out of his desk, adjusted his specs, and said at length:

"Yes, it's quite true, Mr. Waner. You *did* lead the league in triples, doubles, batting average, runs batted in, and runs scored."

Then Barney shifted his eyes to the sacrifice hits column.

"But I see you didn't bunt much," he said emphatically.

JACK MCDONALD

A CASE OF OLD TRICKS

When Branch Rickey instituted his famous five-year plan for the development of the youthful band of athletes he assembled in Pittsburgh, Fred Haney was his manager. The plan ultimately paid off handsomely when the Pirates—almost all of them Branch's boys, although the five-year deadline had not been met and Branch no longer was there—won the pennant in 1960 and defeated the Yankees in the World Series. But that first year was a harrowing one for Haney as his beardless heroes floundered through one dismal game after another.

Late in the season, when he thought he had at least an outside chance to win a game, he sent up a pinch hitter with two out and two on but the boy was in mild panic at finding himself on the spot, and took a third strike. After the game, Branch asked Fred:

"Four years from now, in the same situation, would you call on him?"

"Mr. Rickey," Fred said, "I don't even know where he'll be four years from now and I couldn't hold the game up that long to find out."

F. G.

Casey Stengel had a pretty bad ball club to manage in Brooklyn in 1936 and, on a muggy midsummer afternoon in Boston, it lost a double-header to the Braves, who were almost as bad. On his return to his hotel, Casey went to the barbershop, took off his coat, loosened his tie, opened his shirt collar, and slumped into a chair.

"Give me a shave," he said.

"Anything else?" the barber asked.

"Yes," Casey said, wearily. "Don't cut my throat. I may want to do that later myself."

F. G.

In the spring of 1951 the Yankees, as was their custom at that time, played an exhibition game with the Dodgers at Ebbets Field. A new boy on the club that year was Mickey Mantle, and Casey Stengel said:

"Last year he was a shortstop in Joplin, Missouri, but I got a shortstop by the name of Phil Rizzuto, so I am making an outfielder of Mickey and he is going to play right field. So I take him out there to show him the way the fence is built, starting up straight, then leaning out and finally straightening up again. So, if the right fielder don't know this he is likely to get into trouble because the ball takes many funny spins off this wall. I tell him:

" 'I know this wall very good. I played it for six years.'

"He looks at me in amazement and he says: 'You did?'

"I guess," Casey said, "he thinks I was born at the age of sixty and immediately became the manager of the Yankees."

F. G.

Casey Stengel broke in as an outfielder with the Dodgers in 1912, which was a considerably rougher era in baseball than it ever is likely to know again.

"Nowadays," he said, "if a pitcher gets a ball close to the hitter, the hitter comes back to the bench and says: 'I think he was throwing at me.'

"When I was a young fellow, you knew damned well the pitchers were throwing at you. The first month I was in the league I spent two weeks on my back at the plate."

F. G.

There was a day at the Stadium when the Yankees, although leading the American League as usual, were shot through with injuries, so that Stengel was having a hard time

204

patching together a line-up from his walking wounded. The club was at batting practice and Casey, sitting next to Rizzuto, turned to him and asked:

"What are you talking about?"

"I was just telling Bobby (Brown)," Phil said, "that my wife fell out of bed this morning and—"

"Wait a minute," Casey said.

He called to the other players: "Listen to this."

Then to Phil: "Speak up so they can hear you."

"I was just saying," Phil said, "that my wife was jumping out of bed this morning because the baby was crying and she fell on the floor. She looked so funny I had to laugh. But I felt bad when we found out she'd broken two toes."

"You hear that?" Casey said. "This is a rough season. Even the wives are getting hurt."

F. G.

Bill McKechnie once described baseball as a game of heartbreak for managers. "You can't even celebrate a victory," McKechnie once pointed out. "If you win today, you must start worrying about tomorrow. If you win a pennant, you start worrying about the World Series. As soon as that's over, you start worrying about next season."

LES BIEDERMAN

When Charlie Grimm managed the Braves, they lost a tough game one night in Milwaukee after Danny O'Connell led off an extra inning with a triple and the next three batters couldn't bring him in. The team was due to fly out for New York that night, but when they reached the airport they couldn't find O'Connell.

Grimm beckoned to traveling secretary Duffy Lewis and

suggested: "Better rush back to County Stadium and see if O'Connell is still on third base!"

Les Biederman

When Leo Durocher crosses a hotel lobby, strangers are visibly impressed. Chances are that Leo is every bit as splendid sartorially as the Duke of Windsor, and twice as casual. His fine suit bears the unmistakable stamp of custom tailoring. His accessories are tasteful and exquisitely matched. His shoes bear a high gloss.

People turn to each other and whisper that here, certainly, is a gentleman of formidable means, a scion, possibly, of Mr. Rockefeller. Or even a distant kin to Walter O'Malley. In any case, this is a fat cat.

On two occasions Leo has been named among the best-dressed men in America. Los Angeles merchants once awarded him a plaque for his everyday elegance in haberdashery.

Leo has been fashion conscious since he was a boy of 16 in Springfield, Massachusetts. He worked in the tobacco fields for $6 a day. A tailor in town made suits for $70. Leo saved his money diligently and bought himself a custom set of threads.

Among the Yankees he was known as "Fifth Avenue." Where most rookies owned a pair of pants and a blue serge suit, "Fifth Avenue" promenaded about like Mr. Ruppert himself.

Invited to take inventory one day of the vast collection of wearing apparel that fills the closets of Durocher's Beverly Hills penthouse, we counted 75 suits, 30 sports coats, and 75 pairs of slacks. Lately, he confided, he gets by on only eight new suits a year, tailored by a well-known house in Hollywood at $260 apiece, wholesale plus 10 per cent.

YOU'VE GOT TO BE TAUGHT...

His shirts—naturally monogrammed—are made to order by a French firm and vary in price from $27.50 to $35 apiece, depending upon the material that Leo selects. His shoes, too, are custom-made at $105 a pair, though Durocher assures us they outlast the footwear we step into in ready-made establishments.

With a banker's conservativeness, Leo is repelled by gaudy colors and would sooner drop dead than be found, say, in Argyle socks. Equally repulsive are striped ties. Leo has such strong feelings on flash that his evening wardrobe doesn't even include a white jacket. His six tailored tuxedos all are of black mohair, Durocher's favorite evening material. He also has six topcoats of different weights.

Leo yields to brighter hues only in his sports ensemble. He owns 30 alpaca sweaters—every color in the book.

As an authority on gentlemen's fashions, Durocher was asked how often a guy should change shirts.

"If you aren't a slob," he replied, "you'll use two a day. You wouldn't wear the same shirt in the evening that you wore in the afternoon, would you?"

"What if you can conceal the soiled cuff in the sleeve of your coat?" we inquired.

"You still change at night," Leo insisted.

We didn't ask, but it's safe to assume that Durocher would discourage buffing your shoes on the back of your pants leg, too.

"Do you ever wear a suit two days in a row?" he was asked.

Leo was appalled. "Of course not," he answered. "Never."

"How have you set up your rotation?"

"Most suits, I'd say, work on ten days' rest."

It might be noted quietly that Durocher's theory on undergarments matches that on shirts. You have to admire Leo for his class. How many coaches in baseball wear two pairs of shorts a day?

MEL DURSLAG

During one of the wildest regimes in baseball history, Judge Emil Fuchs bought the Boston Braves and decided to be his own manager.

Joe Dugan, a Yankee immortal, was finishing out the string playing for the Braves. By the wildest of miracles the Braves found themselves tied in the ninth with a man on third. Dugan was at bat. He looked around and trotted back to the bench to tell his manager, "Judge, that kid third baseman of theirs is playing too far back. I'll drop a bunt and we'll squeeze the winning run in."

The Judge was furious. "You'll do no such thing, Mr. Dugan! We'll win fairly or not at all!"

BILL SLOCUM

Mayo Smith, former manager of the Philadelphia Phillies and Cincinnati Reds and now a special assignment man with the New York Yankees, tells of his most embarrassing moment in baseball:

"When I was a minor league outfielder at Toronto, one of my best buddies in the league was Don Ross, then playing third base for Buffalo. We had roomed together at Toronto and were golfing pals.

"One day during a close game between Toronto and Buffalo, I reached third base. Ross called time and walked over to the mound to talk to the pitcher. When he returned, he began a casual conversation with me about golf. Meanwhile, I took a casual lead off third base, with my eyes on

210

the pitcher. Ross edged a little closer to me, then said suddenly: 'Mayo, I bet you never saw a golf ball big as this'—and tagged me out.

"But we're still friends."

FRED RUSSELL

Not long after he became manager of the San Francisco Giants a myth began to encase the person of Alvin Dark. The myth was that, in one way or another, he had appeared in every game of baseball ever played. For example, when Warren Spahn pitched a no-hitter against the Giants, Dark recalled that he had played left field for Milwaukee the day Spahn pitched his previous no-hitter. When plate umpire Augie Donatelli, who had worked Spahn's second no-hitter, remembered that the other no-hit game he'd called balls and strikes in was also against the Giants (Carl Erskine, for Brooklyn, years ago), Dark murmured: "I know. I made the last out."

What had happened was, simply, that Dark had, in the five years before he managed the Giants, played for five different National League teams: Giants, Cardinals, Cubs, Phillies, and Braves. Thus he had it in him to show up at almost any given place at almost any given time.

From this, too, stemmed Dark's league-wide popularity with the fans. He liked to claim perfect memory for names and faces, though obviously no man could recognize everyone among such a legion of well-wishers throughout the league. Alvin persisted, though, in saying he remembered each and every one of them. Finally, one day in St. Louis during the 1961 season, a friend of Dark's determined to put him to the test. A one-armed fan, his right sleeve hanging limp and empty, had hailed Dark by name from the stands, and Alvin had waved cheerily in return.

211

"All right," the friend said. "What's *his* name?"

"Lefty," Dark said. He grinned. "I know them all."

CHARLES EINSTEIN

The most humorous stories I have come into contact with in recent years were the ones Paul Richards told, and still tells, about Frank Gabler, the fellow who was probably last man on the Giant staff in the days when they had Hubbell, Parmelee, Schumacher, Fitzsimmons, etc.

Paul, when he was with the Orioles, had "Gabe"—or "The Great Gabbo," as everybody referred to him—around as often as the directors would be willing to pick up the tab.

Paul would sit around all night and say, "Gabe, tell them about so and so," and of course, Gabe would oblige.

As one story goes, Paul was managing in Atlanta and had Gabe on his staff. They were playing an exhibition game against a major league team and one of the real good pitchers was working against Atlanta.

Anyhow, this guy was just blowing the ball past the Atlanta batters. Now it was the ninth inning and Paul and Gabe were the only two left on the bench who hadn't been in the game.

There was one out and the pitcher would be the fourth man to hit in the inning.

Paul said, "Gabe, if one of the next two guys gets on, one of us is going to have to pinch hit." (Gabe was a good hitting pitcher.)

So Gabe said, "Hell, Paul, I might as well get a bat, because I know you ain't gonna hit against this guy."

Sure enough, the next hitter walked, and Gabe got up with two out and a man on first.

212

Steamboat Johnson, the famous old Southern League umpire, was behind the plate.

The first pitch came in at about 100 miles an hour, and Gabe fell away from the plate and took it. Steamboat said, "Steerika one!" The next one was an exploding curve and Gabe was down on one knee. Steamboat said, "Steeeerika two—right down Broadway—and he knew it."

The next pitch was a sidearm curve and Gabe wound up on hands and knees, and Paul says he reached for his bat and glove and started to head for the clubhouse, because the pitch looked right down the middle.

For some reason, Steamboat said, "Ball," and from his knees, Gabe looked up and said, "Steamer, call 'em right. You're just delaying the game."

Apparently, Gabler used to draw the assignment against Van Lingle Mungo when the Giants played Brooklyn, because Hubbell would just have pitched against one of the better clubs before they got into Brooklyn, and the other starters would come up with some kind of ailment because they wanted to duck Mungo, the only tough pitcher the Dodgers had. According to Paul, Gabe gave Mungo some good battles.

In one close game, the Giants had a man on first with one out and Gabe at the bat. Terry debated whether to put on the sacrifice or let Gabe swing, because, as I say, he was a good hitter. This day Mungo was really humming. Terry walked up to the plate and said, "Gabe, do you think you can hit this guy to right?"

There was a pause and Gabe said, "Waal, Will, the way I figure, if I hit 'er at all she'll go to right."

I've heard this story attributed to other people, but Richards says Gabe was the original.

He was coaching at third one day at Atlanta and somebody hit a double with a man on first. Gabe waved the runner all the way, and from the start was yelling, "Come on."

He said "Come on" when the guy hit second, "Come on" when he got near third and, when he hit the bag, waved him home and said "Go ahead." Just then the relay man made a hell of a throw and Gabe said, "Yeah, go ahead you so-and-so, but I don't believe you're gonna make it."

He didn't either.

During Gabe's years with the Giants, Hubbell was practically unbeatable. He rarely was knocked out of the box. One day, though, he didn't have it, and Terry decided to take him out after he had been knocked around pretty good.

He brought Gabler in from the bullpen and when he got to the mound for the little conference, Terry gave him the old routine.

"Do you think you can get this guy out for me, Gabe?" he asked.

Gabe said, "Who you kiddin', Will? If the King—the greatest pitcher in baseball—can't get these guys out, how do you expect me to get 'em out? If you want me to pitch, give me the ball, but don't be expecting me to do something Hubbell can't do."

One local incident that comes to mind is the one in which the final out of the game was called with the ball lying in the middle of the infield.

The Orioles were behind about three runs in the ninth during the dog days when victories were extremely rare. Joe Taylor, never exactly an Einstein, singled with one out and nobody on, and for some reason known only to himself, tried to stretch an ordinary single into a double.

Al Kaline threw the ball in to second, and Taylor was out by at least ten feet. Coot Veal reached for the ball and

214

went down with the tag. Bill Summers went up with the out sign, turned his back, and headed for the dugout with the rest of the umpires.

Taylor jumped up screaming, and Al Vincent, the first-base coach, did likewise. What everybody, including 10,000 people in the stands, saw was that Veal never did catch the ball. It rolled about halfway to the mound and stopped in full view of everybody. Frank Bolling trotted in from second base, sheepishly leaned over and scooped up the ball, and continued into the dugout. The game was over, but the fellow who supposedly made the tag for the final out didn't have the ball.

Another strange play occurred on Kluszewski's controversial home run. Milt Pappas came into the top of the eighth protecting a 2-run lead. With 2 on, Al Lopez sent Big Klu up as a pinch hitter. At the same time he sent a reliefer to the bullpen on a rush call. Instead of going all the way to the bullpen, the pitcher and catcher stopped about ten feet from the home plate and started hurriedly playing catch.

As Pappas wound up, Ed Hurley (the third-base umpire) called time, because he spotted the two warming up short of the bullpen. Nobody in the stands and few of the players heard him call time. Pappas made the pitch and Klu hit a low screamer into the right-field seats. While he was giving it the Cadillac treatment going around the bases, Brooks Robinson looked like a helicopter at third, trying to make everybody realize Hurley had called time. Klu got almost to third before he heard the news, and as was to be expected, he was fit to be tied. Anyhow, he had to hit over, and this time he lined out to right. Pappas stopped them after that and won the game.

It was one of the few times I have ever seen Hurley sorry

he had stuck his nose into a play. He admitted he was sorry
he had made the call, but there was nothing he could do
once he had opened his mouth.

BOB MAISEL

Frank Lane, when working, is an energetic, headstrong
individual who will keep going around the clock, if he
needs to.

It was well after midnight one night while he was general
manager of the Cleveland Indians that he decided to go to
his office. He banged on the door of the Cleveland Stadium
until finally a watchman came along. He asked the identity
of his late caller and Frank told him.

"I can't let you in," was the surprising reply.

Frank fumed, as he can easily do.

"I'm the general manager of this club," he roared.

"Ha! ha!" came the answer. "I don't care who you are—
I can't let you in."

"You can't?" Lane exclaimed. "Why can't you let me in?"

"Because the blankety-blank key is stuck in the so-and-so
lock!" the night watchman replied.

For once in his life, Frank had no comeback.

LEO FISCHER

Fights among ballplayers usually are all sound and fury
and nobody gets hurt. But Charlie Grimm remembers one
in which he was a principal that, as far as he was concerned,
was no laughing matter.

"It took place at old Baker Bowl in Philadelphia," he
said. "I was young and with the Pirates and not as smart as
I am now or I wouldn't have got involved in it. Anyway,
Carson Bigbee and Rabbit Maranville and I got to yelling

216

back and forth during the game with Irish Meusel and Mack Wheat of the Phillies. Remember Mack? He's Zack Wheat's brother and he was a catcher. Well, we said we would see them under the stand after the ball game, and we kept the appointment and found ourselves in a tangle of posts and girders.

"I was dodging around among the posts, trying to get a poke at somebody and I saw Bigbee swing at Meusel. He missed and Wheat hit him back of the ear and it sounded like a guy hitting a bass drum, and Bigbee went down. Just then Meusel came charging around the post nearest to me and hit me in the mouth and I went down, too. I don't know who hit Maranville but he was on the ground when I got there. There we were, the three of us, laid out and those two Philadelphia guys standing over us in fighting position, waiting for us to get up so they could knock us down again. They could have waited all night for me because that punch in the mouth had cured me and I didn't want to fight any more, but by that time the cops came swarming in and, when I thought it was good and safe, I got up."

F. G.

Peahead Walker is better known as a coach in college and professional football, but for years he played or managed in the minor baseball leagues, mainly in the South. In 1937 he was the pilot of the Snow Hill club in the Coastal Plains League. Peahead tells it this way:

"Mr. Exum owned the club. He also owned the general store in the town. He and I became great friends and after every home game we won I'd go down to the store and we'd sit in the back and he'd pour whiskey out of a big jug and we'd have a nice time. But he was such a fan and felt so bad when we lost that when I'd get down to the store I'd find

217

the door closed and with a big padlock on it. I'd know he was in there, all right, but he wouldn't let on that he was and I'd have to go some place else to get a drink to console myself with.

"We had a catcher on our club named Aaron Robinson. I know you remember him. He was such a stickout in our league it was a cinch that somebody from the big leagues would come looking at him and one day Mr. Weiss of the Yankees showed up. Seems like Paul Krichell or Gene McCann or one of his other scouts had seen the boy and he was impressed by the report on him and even more impressed when he saw him. After the game—we won that day—Mr. Exum and Mr. Weiss and I went down to the store and went in the back room and Mr. Exum got out the jug. After a while, Mr. Weiss says:

" 'I'd like to talk to you about Robinson.'

" 'I can guess what you'll have to say,' Mr. Exum says. 'How much will you give for him?'

" '$5,000,' George says.

"That puts a strange light in Mr. Exum's eyes and I says to him:

" 'Just a moment. If Mr. Weiss will excuse us, I'd like to talk to you.'

"Mr. Weiss says it is all right with him, so we go into another room and I says to him:

" 'Look, Mr. Exum. Mr. Weiss wants this boy and if we handle it right we can get more than $5,000 for him. I should have told you before to start out by asking $25,000 and then retreat from there, if you have to. I'm sure if you play it right you can get $10,000 anyway.'

" 'Peahead,' he says to me, 'all my life I've been selling things. I've sold horses and cows and hogs and groceries. I've sold blankets and dress goods and rope and kerosene
218

oil—but I never before had a chance to sell a man. So when we go back there with Mr. Weiss, please don't say anything that might spoil this deal.'

"So," Peahead said, "that's how it come about that the Yankees got Aaron Robinson for $5,000."

F. G.

On a morning late in the season of 1926, a 16-year-old boy, clutching a straw suitcase and obviously scared, showed up at the players' gate at the Polo Grounds. He wanted to see Mr. McGraw, he told Willis, the gatetender. Mr. Williams, a friend of Mr. McGraw's in Louisiana, had written to Mr. McGraw about him and Mr. McGraw had said to send him up.

"I'm a ballplayer," the boy nervously told Willis. "I'm a catcher."

Willis, who didn't often smile when on duty—this also was the press and general pass gate and he had to be on guard constantly against crashers—smiled now as he opened the barrier.

Such was the beginning of the great and wonderful career of Melvin Thomas Ott. It was to end on a shocking note on July 16, 1948.

The setting was the Giants' office on West 42nd Street and Horace Stoneham announced that Ott had been released and that his successor was Leo Durocher. The crowded office boiled with excitement, as newspapermen milled about, telephones jangled, everybody talked at once. Garry Schumacher, director of promotions for the club, said:

"I guess we'd better be going."

The Giants had gone to Pittsburgh to open a series and

Horace and Garry were flying out with Durocher to present him to the players as their new manager.

"So long," Ott said to Leo. "Good luck—and say good-by to the fellows for me."

"Thanks, Mel," Leo said. "Sure. Sure."

The group was beginning to break up.

"You'll be around for a while, won't you, Mel?" one of them asked.

"Yes," he said. "I don't know for how long. You know I'm going to be Hubbell's assistant in the farm system and I'll do a lot of traveling. But I'll be here for a little while, I expect."

"Well, see you at Shor's."

"Fine," Mel said. "I'll be seeing you."

He was very close to tears.

F. G.

Branch Rickey is celebrated for, among his other skills, his ability to negotiate salary disputes with his ballplayers and the belief is that no holdout, however redoubtable, ever took a decision over him.

"One of his defenses," Joe Garagiola said, "was especially effective against young players, who thought they should get $500—or $5,000—more than Branch offered. He would so impress them with the fact that the possession of too much money imposed a dreadful responsibility upon them that he'd have them worrying about money they didn't have— and from there on they didn't have a chance."

Branch had a rather amusing session, although not along that line, with Rube Melton, a pitcher, whom he had obtained from the Phillies in the winter of 1942-43. All Rube needed was a lesson in arithmetic and he got it, you may be sure. He had returned his contract, unsigned, and Branch

PIN (STRIPE) MONEY

invited him to Brooklyn from his home in Cramerton, North Carolina, at the club's expense.

"What don't you like about this contract?" Branch asked.

"I got more money than that last year," Melton said.

"I beg your pardon. You got $3,500 last year and I am offering you $5,000."

"I got $5,300 last year."

Branch had before him a copy of Rube's 1942 contract.

"It doesn't say that here," he said.

"It ain't in the contract."

"Did you have a verbal agreement for a bonus?"

"Not exactly."

"So?"

"Well, last spring they fined me $100. A couple of weeks later they give it back to me. That was a hundred extra."

"Now, wait a minute! Do you mean to tell me that if I take $100 out of this pocket and put it in this one I have gained $100?"

"All I know is, I got the money."

Branch regarded him with astonishment for a moment. Then:

"All right. Now, according to your way of figuring, you have made $3,600. Is that right?"

"Yes."

"Then?"

"In June they give me $500."

"What for?"

"They just give it to me."

Branch picked up his telephone and called Gerry Nugent, president of the Phillies.

"Why did you give Melton $500 last June?" he asked.

"I didn't give it to him," Nugent said. "I loaned it to him."

"Thank you, Gerry," he said, and put down the receiver. Turning to Melton, he said:

"Now you have made $4,100. Is that correct?"

"Yes."

"And the balance?"

"Well, in August I needed a little money and—"

"And Nugent advanced it to you?"

"That's right."

"Suppose you take a walk for a half hour or so, Rube," Branch said, "and while you're walking think over my offer of $5,000."

When Rube returned, he still acted as though he was being badly treated, but he signed the contract.

Branch sometimes used the rawest kind of flattery as a lure for the brash seekers of gold. For example, he telephoned one of them who had remained obdurate even after the other players had reported for spring practice and said:

"This is Mr. Rickey. I am at the training camp. Don't you think you should be here?"

"I ain't moving until I get the money I want," the athlete said.

"Money! Money! Is that all you think about? Have you no pride in the Brooklyn club? Wait! Don't answer! Have you no regard for your fellow players? Do you realize they are here every day, toiling hard to get in shape, their minds and hearts set on winning the pennant?"

"Yeah. I know all about that."

"But do you know they look for you every day?"

"No."

"That they ask for you? That they know they need you if they are to win the pennant?"

"They do?"

"Yes! And do you know I have given them my promise

224

you will be here? And that, moreover, I have promised the newspapermen you will come and that nine photographers were here today looking for you?"

"They were? Nine photographers? Looking for me?"

"Yes. . . . Now will you come?"

"I'm starting tomorrow, boss!"

"That's a good boy," Branch said. "And when you get here we will look over your contract again."

He hung up and turned to his secretary, Mel Jones.

"Mel," he said," see if you can round up nine photographers from somewhere—anywhere—to come here for a few days. I have an idea I may need them."

F. G.

"Managing a ball club," Birdie Tebbetts once said, "is a job for which a man works, studies, hopes and, if he's gaited that way, prays—knowing all the time that if he gets it he's bound, in the end, to be fired."

In the last torturous weeks in Cincinnati, where he'd been hailed as a hero and had done an excellent job until a sudden decline which was no fault of his, and when the club was out of town, he was hanged in effigy by irate fans in Fountain Square. When he heard of this, he said, with characteristic grace:

"I don't blame them. If I had been there, I would have lent a hand on the rope.

"Baseball is a gripping thing," Birdie went on. "You play it in the spring, summer, and early fall. And think about it all winter, when the snow is on the ground in New Hampshire, where I live. That is, you do if you are a manager. One winter night in my time as manager of the Reds, my wife and I were sitting in front of the fireplace, the children having been put to bed and all being quiet in the house. My wife was reading and I was sitting there, watching the logs burn down and thinking back to the games we'd lost but might have won during the past season, when Mrs. Tebbetts looked up from her book and asked:

" 'What inning are we in?'

"That same winter—and along the same line—Mrs. Tebbetts and I were in New York and one night I met Red Smith in a theater lobby, where we'd gone for a smoke between acts.

" 'How's your progeny?' he asked.

"And I said: 'Pretty good. But I'd feel better if I had another good right-handed hitter in the outfield and another good left-handed pitcher.'

"He looked at me a little strangely but didn't say anything, and it wasn't until I got back to my seat that I realized I had mistaken his 'progeny' for 'prodigies,' and I said to myself:

" 'Red must think I'm daffier than I really am.' "

F. G.

Early in September of 1929 Miller Huggins knew that the Yankees, who had won the pennant in 1926, 1927, and 1928 and the World Series, each in four games, in '27 and '28, were not going to win again. It wasn't only that the Philadelphia Athletics, under Connie Mack, had reached a peak and snatched the lead from them. Collectively, save for Babe Ruth, who would wind up the season with 46 home runs and a batting average of .345, they were in a rut from which he could not free them.

There was an afternoon at the Stadium when, after another lost game, he sat with Colonel Jacob Ruppert and Ed Barrow and Jake asked anxiously:

"What's the matter with the boys, Hug?"

226

"They're through, Colonel," Hug said.

"But we still have a month—"

"Forget about it," Hug said. "Start getting ready for next year. These fellows are through."

"How do you know?" Jake asked.

"I just finished talking to them. I talked to them calmly. I pleaded with them. Then I abused them. It didn't make the slightest difference. I couldn't make them mad. I couldn't even make them laugh. When I realized I might just have been talking to that wall over there, I quit."

"But why? Why should they be through?"

"I guess they're just tired," Hug said. "I'm tired myself. I'm tired out . . . and I can't sleep."

For some years the Little Miller had suffered from neuritis. Now his condition was aggravated by his worries as the Yankees faltered in their pursuit of the Athletics.

On September 20, when he met with his coaches, Arthur Fletcher and Charlie O'Leary, in the clubhouse an hour or so before game time, there was an ugly red blotch under his left eye.

"I must have picked up some kind of infection," he said.

"It looks like a boil to me," Charlie said. "Why don't you go home and take it easy and then see a doctor?"

"You don't think I'd trust the ball club to a couple of clowns like you, do you?" he asked, with a forced and gentle smile.

But just before game time, in the dugout, he said to Fletcher:

"Art, I'm going home. Look after the ball club."

He dressed and walked out of the Stadium for the last time. The "infection" was a carbuncle and the poison spread so rapidly through his system that, on September 25, he died.

They were a hard-boiled crew, the Yankees of 1929, but

227

they cried in the clubhouse when they heard that he would not come their way again. The Babe, Lou Gehrig, Tony Lazzeri, and some of the other regulars accompanied him on his last journey to Cincinnati for burial in Woodlawn Cemetery. Lazzeri was so affected by Hug's death that he did not play again that year but went from Cincinnati to his home in San Francisco.

F. G.

This was the night of July 5, 1946. The Giants were playing the Dodgers at the Polo Grounds. In the Dodgers' dugout before the game, Red Barber was needling Leo Durocher, then the manager, about the home runs the Giants had hit the day before.

"Home runs!" Leo said. "Some home runs! Line drives and pop flies that would have been caught on a bigger field! That's what they were!"

"Why don't you admit they were real home runs?" Red asked. "Why don't you be a nice guy for a change?"

Leo had been reclining on the bench. Now he leaped to his feet.

"A nice guy!" he yelled. "A nice guy! I been around baseball for a long time and I've known a lot of nice guys."

He walked up and down the dugout, then whirled and pointed to the Giants' dugout.

"Nice guys!" he said. "Look over there. Do you know a nicer guy than Mel Ott? Or any of the other Giants? Why, they're the nicest guys in the world! And where are they? In last place!"

He walked up and down again, beating himself on the chest.

"Nice guys! I'm not a nice guy—and I'm in first place. Nobody helped me to get there, either, except the guys on

228

this ball club and they ain't nice guys! There wasn't anybody in this league helped me to get there. They saw me coming up and they—"

He stamped on the floor of the dugout.

"That's what they gave me!" he yelled. "Nobody said to me, 'You're in third place now, Leo. We want to see you get up to second.' "

He picked a towel from the bench and held it high and patted it and said: "Nobody said, 'You're in second place now, Leo. We'd like to see you in first place.' "

He threw the towel back on the bench.

"No, sir! Nobody wanted to see me up there. All the nice guys in the league wanted to knock me down, which is the way it should be. But in spite of them, I got up there. I'm in first place now and—"

He waved a hand toward the Giant dugout.

"The nice guys are over there in last place. Well, let them come and get me!"

The Dodgers were at batting practice and Eddie Stanky was at the plate.

"Look at that little ———!" Leo said. "Think he's a nice guy? The hell he is! He'll knock you down to make a play if he has to. That's the kind of guys I want on my ball club."

He spoke warmly now.

"Look at him," he said. "The little ———. He can't run, he can't hit, he can't throw, he can't do nothing. But what a ballplayer! I wouldn't give him for any second baseman in the league. Or for any two second basemen."

The bell rang and the Dodgers were streaming into the dugout. A reporter who had been sitting on the bench got up.

"All right, boys," he said. "Make room for some nice guys."

"Not in this dugout," Leo said.

229

He waved toward the Giants' dugout again.

"The nice guys are all over there," he said. "In last place."

F. G.

Many factors, of course, entered into the introduction and development of baseball in Japan but no individual contributed to it to a greater degree than Frank ("Lefty") O'Doul. As manager of the San Francisco Seals in the Pacific Coast League, he made annual tours of that country with his team and between exhibition games devoted much of his time to coaching high school and college players. He thus became the most popular American sports figure in the land and his team the most celebrated, and so it happened....

Well, there was this small boy in a family that had been converted to Catholicism and, when he was about to be confirmed, chose St. Francis de Sales as his confirmation name. But when the great moment was at hand and the bishop asked him how he wished to be called, he said:

"San Francisco Seals!"

F. G.

This was a spring in St. Petersburg, where the Yankees were training, and Babe Ruth had just met with Colonel Jacob Ruppert and signed a contract calling for a salary of $70,000. That night, at a dinner given for Ruppert by the baseball writers, the Babe told of his first contract with the Baltimore club of the International League for $1,500. Ruppert sighed and shook his head.

"What's the matter, Colonel?" the Babe asked.

"I was just thinking," Ruppert said, "that that's when I should have known you."

F. G.

The late George Stallings, the "Miracle Man" who drove the Boston Braves from last place on the Fourth of July to the pennant in 1914 and then to a World Series victory over the heavily favored Philadelphia Athletics in four games, suffered a mild heart attack on a train bound for his home in Brunswick, Georgia, at the end of the season a year or two later. The conductor found a doctor on the train and the doctor, entering George's drawing room, found him sitting up, gazing out the window. Having satisfied himself that the attack had passed and that George was in no immediate danger, but wanting to know something of the history of the case, he asked:

"What do you suppose was the origin of your condition, Mr. Stallings?"

And George, still gazing out the window, said:

"Bases on balls."

F. G.

X. Fans

The hard hat fan passed out with the hard hat, meaning the derby. He wore a white shirt with no collar—this was in the era of detachable collars—and a derby and sat in the bleachers. He knew more about baseball than the swells in the grandstand and was objective in his thinking.

There was one in the left-field bleachers at the Polo Grounds in the long ago when Fred Clarke was the manager and left-fielder of the Pirates and had a youngster named Max Carey in center field. Carey (now in the Hall of Fame) brought off a couple of good plays and one of the left-field bleacher mob yelled to the veteran Clarke:

"Why don't you watch that kid and learn how to play the outfield?"

At that, a hard hat stood up and, addressing the heckler, said sharply:

"Don't ever do that again! Don't ever criticize a manager in the hearing of one of his ballplayers!"

A hard hat also could have a sense of humor. As, for instance, one at the old Hilltop grounds in New York where the Highlanders, later to become known as the Yankees, played. It was a Fourth of July and broiling, and before the game, a bosomy contralto from the Metropolitan Opera Company took her place at the plate to sing "The Star-Spangled Banner."

Everybody stood up, naturally and, when she had finished the first verse, everybody sat down. But she launched into the second verse. Up came the crowd again, down it went again, when she'd sung the last line of it. But there she still stood and, as she raised her voice in the third verse, a hard hat bawled:

"Why don't somebody give that broad a base on balls?"

F. G.

The first year that Ted Sullivan was associated with Chris Von Der Ahe at St. Louis, Chris had a board of directors who were a lot of cranks who had baseball on the brain, and they were often interfering with his management. One day Sullivan told Von Der Ahe he didn't propose to be dictated to by a bunch of fanatics.

"Vot dat you call it? Fans?" Chris asked.

"Yes, fans, for short. They are a lot of fans," Sullivan replied. The members of the St. Louis team, who heard about this from Sullivan, then adopted the term.

In the Texas League in 1888 there were numerous former members of the Browns. They used the word "fan" to describe a baseball enthusiast or crank. The word was then used in print, in *The Sporting News* by Ren Mulford, the Cincinnati writer, in 1888.

LEE ALLEN

Once there was a writer who made a spot check of four leading hitters in the American League at the time and was

233

surprised at the variety of answers he got to his question, which was:

"What is the secret of hitting?"

"It's in the eyes," Babe Ruth said. "If you can't see the ball good, you can't hit it."

"It's in the stance," said George Burns, the slugging first baseman of the Indians. "If you're not comfortable up there, it means you're out of line and you can't hit the ball solidly."

"It's the stroke," said Harry Heilmann, of the Tigers, three-time batting champion of the league. "Baseball is like every game played with a stick and a ball—golf, billiards, tennis, for instance. When your stroke is off, you're out of luck. The only batting practice really worth anything is that which you get in spring training. That's when you adjust your stroke after a winter's idleness."

"There's no secret to it," said Bob ("Fat") Fothergill of the Tigers. "You just go up there and belt the ball. What the hell is secret about that?"

F. G.

New York fans traditionally are the most sporting. An illustrative incident is the time Bill Terry, rather newly come to the Giants, belted a long ball to center that looked as if it might be the first ever to go into the bleachers in a regular game. Rounding second, he heard a tremendous roar and he began jogging plateward, figuring he had a homer—only to learn that the roar was for a sensational catch Lloyd Waner of the Pirates had made on him. Terry couldn't get over a home-town crowd being so lavish in its praise for an enemy player—a situation that prevails even today in New York and probably nowhere else.

MEL HEIMER

There was this game between the Dodgers and the Cardinals when Rogers Hornsby was at his peak. The Cardinals had clubbed the starting pitcher out of sight and now there was a rookie in there in relief and when Hornsby came up, the kid asked Jack Fournier, the Dodgers' first baseman:

"How should I pitch to him?"

"A fast ball on the inside," Fournier said.

The young man followed instructions and Hornsby blasted a double past the third baseman.

"I thought you said he couldn't hit a fast ball inside!" the rookie exclaimed.

"I didn't say that," Fournier said. "I got a wife and family to think about and I don't want that ———— hitting an outside pitch my way."

F. G.

Johnny Allen out of Lenoir, North Carolina—he was with the Yankees, the Indians, the Browns, the Dodgers and, ultimately, the Giants—hated hitters more than most pitchers ever did and feuded with them constantly.

"Is it true," someone asked him when he was at his violent best, "that if your grandmother went to bat against you in a clutch you would knock her down?"

Johnny had a sense of humor when he wasn't pitching.

"Well," he said, with a crooked smile, "I don't guess I'd go that far. But I sure as hell wouldn't give her a good ball to hit."

F. G.

There are, well, speaking conservatively, a million stories about Jay Kirke, who bounced around in the minor leagues for a long time, went up to the majors and went down again but, wherever he was, could tear the hide off a baseball with

235

his bat but too often didn't know what to do with one when he found it in his glove at or near first base when one or more runners were on the paths. Like unto all good hitters, he was proud of his prowess and this is the best-known story they tell of him. The locale? It really doesn't make any difference. It could have been Detroit or Boston or Cleveland, or any of the towns that knew him in the American Association. At any rate, he was a recent bridegroom and when he'd get home after a game—this was before night baseball—his bride would have dinner well on the way toward the table and, proud of the big man as he was of himself, would ask:

"Well, my honey, well, my bee, how many hits today?"

And he would say: "A double, two singles, and a home run."

Or: "Two doubles and two singles."

(He never made—well, almost never made—a triple. He couldn't run that fast.)

But this was a day when, in four times at bat, he hadn't hit a ball out of the infield and his mood was bleak. As usual, his bride asked:

"Well, my honey, well, my bee, how many hits today?"

And Jay snarled: "Look here! You tend to the cookin' and I'll do the hittin'!"

F. G.

Away back in the dim dead yonder I thought I was quite a ballplayer—semiprofessionally, that is. I led a club in St. Joseph, Missouri, called the Eagles. It was called the Eagles because through a brother of mine who was secretary of the St. Joseph chapter of the Fraternal Order of Eagles we were staked to uniforms and occasionally given expense money for trips.

We didn't disgrace the order. We had a pretty sharp record. I was an infielder and rotated between third and short. I will admit my hitting was not too hot but occasionally I would hit one in a pinch.

Once we played a game against a crack outfit in some Kansas town. The Kansas pitcher had more on the ball than I had ever looked at before. They beat us. We could hardly get a man on base. The man, or boy, pitching against us was Fred Glade. He later became famous with the old St. Louis Browns and, I think, held the strikeout record with 18.

Despite my weak hitting, old Jack Holland, then managing St. Joseph—or St. Joe, as we called it—took a chance on me. He tried me out in spring training and then gave me a berth as utility when the season opened. I sat on the bench most of the time but once St. Joe was playing Denver. At that time those two teams were battling for the lead. Cy Falkenberg, later a famous Cleveland star, was pitching for Denver. Jack Hendricks was managing Denver at the time.

Rabbit Powell, who later was an outfield star with the Boston Braves, smacked out a single over the second baseman's head. Holland looked around the bench. He spied me.

"Think you can hit one?" he asked. My heart sank into my shoes but I put on an act and called out in a loud voice, "Sure."

"Get a stick and get in there," growled Jack.

I did and marched up to the plate. Falkenberg looked ten feet tall. The first ball came whizzing down from out of the sky and cut the plate and I stood right there with the bat on my shoulder. That happened twice more and I started back to the bench. Now I think of that line Tim Hurst used to pull: "You can't get a hit with the bat on your shoulder." He always pulled that when someone beefed about a strike call without having swung.

That walk back to the bench was the longest I ever took in my life. And, as I note that ballplayers still do, I went over to the water cooler and took myself a long drink. And I stood there a long time. I didn't want to face Holland. But he forgave me and later I saw considerable action. But my batting average remains a secret.

BARRY FARIS

One of the greatest hitters in baseball history was Jesse Burkett—three times he topped the .400 mark back around the turn of the century—and he was also quite a character.

A crabbing, hotheaded character, always with a chip on his shoulder for the umpires.

Seldom could a big league umpire cool Jesse off. And never could he be cooled off by a New England League arbiter later when he was the owner, manager, and ace pinch hitter of the club that represented his home town of Worcester.

But there came a day when he just had to cool himself off—a steaming August dog day at Ocean Park in Lynn—and that he did in style most spectacular as Worcester was trailing Lynn by all of 12–0 in the ninth inning.

Hot all over was old Jesse, not just in the head, when he arose from the bench and growled to his horse-collared hirelings:

"I'll show you blind bums how to hit that ball! And I'll show you something else, too, after I hit it."

Then he reported to the umpire: "Burkett battin' for Exercise."

Jesse still had his supersharp batting eye, it should be told, and he'd never lost any portion of that which he called "the old confeedience."

But he couldn't run at this stage of his career, alas, what

with a potbelly along with other weight for age and a creaking pair of legs.

"Waddle I Do" would have been the song for the old boy had he ever been in a singing mood on heading for first base after adding another to his countless number of safe hits.

Yes, he was strictly a waddler now.

Well, Jesse pointed toward left center when he dug in at the Ocean Park plate—he could call his shots often in that league—and a few seconds later he lined out right out there to where he'd pointed.

A soft sort of two-bagger it looked to be, even for spavined, slow-footed Jesse.

But he had his own ideas.

Beyond right field, through an open horse-and-buggy gate in the fence, could be seen the cool and inviting Atlantic. And that, rather than second base, was the sweltering veteran's goal.

No turn at first base for Jesse on this day.

On a straight line he kept waddling, through the horse-and-buggy gate, and he didn't stop waddling until he took a dive into the ocean, uniform and all.

He'd had that refreshing dip in mind, you see, even before he left the bench to get up there and bat for Exercise.

JIMMY DOYLE

Of all the Brooklynese remarks during ball games, which are legend, I personally always liked the one that one fan roared at Whit Wyatt, pitching against the Giants: "T'row it down his t'roat, Whit!"

MEL HEIMER

239

XI. Slanguage

Slanguage is as American as Ticonderoga and Gettysburg. It is the seasoning of speech. Every walk in life—each category in business and labor, in professions, in the military world, in sports, etc.—has its own slang expressions. Even baseball.

Here is a glossary of jargon as used by ballplayers on and off the field:

ANNIE OAKLEY: free ticket.

ARLIE LATHAM: a third baseman lifting a leg to avoid being struck on the shin by a hard-hit ball.

AROUND THE HORN: sidearm curve to batter when the count is 3 and 2; also double play, third to second to first.

ASH HEAP: rough infield.

AUTOMATIC STRIKE: the pitch on a 3 and 0 count (but not necessarily to a hard hitter).

BACKSTOP: a catcher.

BAD HANDS: a player with a poor fielding average.

BAG: first, second or third base.

BALTIMORE CHOP: a batted ball that hits the plate and bounces high into the air.

BALLOON: a soft pitch.

BEANBALL: a pitch that is aimed at the batter's head.

240

BEARING DOWN: a pitcher making his best effort.

BELLY WHOPPER: a slide into a base head first.

BENCHED: a player kept out of a game, perhaps for poor hitting, or taken out for some tactical reason.

BINGLE: a base hit.

BLOOPER: an accidental hit over the infield.

BLOW: a safe hit.

BONEHEAD: a particularly dumb player.

BONER: a stupid play.

BOOK: information compiled on a player or a club.

BOMBED: hit hard.

BREAKING STUFF: curve balls.

BRUSHBACK: a pitch designed to keep a hitter from crowding the plate.

BOOT: an error.

BOX CAR TOWN: very small town.

BROADWAY: a swell dresser.

BUG: a baseball fan.

BULLPEN: spot on field where relief pitchers warm up.

BUNT: to meet the ball with a loosely held bat so that it will go only a short distance.

BUSHER: a minor-leaguer.

BUTTERFLY BALL: a pitch that floats over the plate like a butterfly.

CAN OF CORN: a high, lazy fly ball.

CHANGE OF PACE: a slow pitch delivered with the same motion as a fast ball.

CIRCUIT DRIVE: a home run.

CIRCUS CATCH: difficult catch.

CLEANUP BATTER: fourth man in the batting order.

CLOTHESLINE DRIVE: a hit that speeds out at a low level.

COUSIN: a pitcher easy for a hitter.

CROOKED ARM: a left-handed pitcher.

CUP OF COFFEE: a short stay with a big-league club.

CYCLOPS: any player who wears glasses.

DAISY SCORCHER: a safe hit to the outfield on or near the ground.

DANIEL WEBSTER: player who looks wise; good arguer.

DERRICK: removal of a pitcher from the mound, usually for giving up too many hits.

DIAMOND: the rectangular space in which the game of baseball is played.

DICK SMITH: a sneak drinker.

DOWN THE ALLEY: a perfect strike.

DREAMER: a player who isn't paying attention on the field.

DROP ONE: to place a bunt.

DUCKS ON THE POND: runners on base.

DUSTER: a pitch designed to drive a batter back and away from plate.

EAGLE CLAW: glove.

EARLY SHOWER: said of a player kicked out of the game by the umpire.

FAN: an enthusiastic follower of the game (from fanatic).

FAR CORNER: third base.

FAT ONE: a pitch right down the middle, easy for a batter.

FIND THE HANDLE: when a player makes a gross error in the field he "can't find the handle" of the ball.

FIREMAN: a relief pitcher who is effective.

FOOT IN THE BUCKET: said of a batter whose rear foot is outside the chalk line.

FOUR MASTER: a home run.

FOUR FOR 0: four times at bat, no hit.

FRONT-RUNNER: a player or team in the lead.

GET A JUMP: make a quick start toward the next base as the pitcher begins his motion toward the plate.

GET THE GATE: kicked off the playing field by the umpire.

GILLETTE: ball thrown at batter's head—scraping his whiskers.

GLASS ARM: a weak throwing arm.

GRANDSTAND MANAGER: a baseball fan who second-guesses the manager.

GRAPEFRUIT LEAGUE: spring training games.

HASSOCK: refers to a base.

HE TOOK A DRINK: headed for water cooler after striking out.

HIGH HARD ONE: a high fast ball.

HIT IN A PINCH: a hit at the right moment with runners on base.

HOGAN'S BACK YARD: rough diamond.

HORSE-AND-BUGGY LEAGUE: a minor league, whose players ride on buses.

HOT CORNER: third base.

242

IRON MIKE: a pitching machine.
INITIAL SACK: first base.
IVORY: high-priced rookie.
JESSE JAMES: any umpire.
JUNK MAN: a pitcher who throws only slow balls of varying speeds and also curves.
KEYSTONE SACK: second base.
LEADOFF MAN: the first man in the line-up or first at bat in an inning.
LAY IT DOWN: to bunt.
LEATHER MAN: a good fielder.
LONG STRIKE: a foul ball.
MANICURIST: groundkeeper.
MEAL TICKET: a constantly effective pitcher.
MOXIE: a player's guts or know-how shown in a game.
NAPPING: a player when caught off a base.
NIGHTCAP: the second game of a double-header.
NUBBER: a lucky base hit.
ON DECK: awaiting a turn to get in the batter's box.
ONE-CUSHION SHOT: line drive bouncing off the wall, usually for extra bases.
PAN: home plate.
PASS: base on balls.
PICKPOCKET: signal stealer.
PINCH HITTER: a player who substitutes for a man scheduled to come up to the plate.
PLOW JOCKEY: a farm boy.
POOL TABLE: a smooth infield.
POWDER THE BALL: to hit it hard.
PUNCH THE BAG: to talk.
PUT SOME MUSTARD ON IT: put extra speed on a pitched ball.
RABBIT EARS: player who hears and is upset by the fans' jeers.
RHUBARB: a boisterous argument on the playing field.
ROUNDHOUSE: a pitch with a wide outcurve.
RUBINOFF: star always in need of a haircut.
SACRIFICE: a short grounder to advance a man on base.
SACRIFICE FLY: a fly ball long enough to score a runner from third base.
SAFETY: a safe hit.

SAW THE BARRELS: passed a barrel wagon, taken as an omen of good luck.

SAILER: a fast pitch that sails.

SCATTER-ARM: a fielder who habitually throws wildly.

SINKER: a pitched ball that drops sharply; a batted ball that does the same.

SLUGGER: a heavy hitter.

SMOKE: speed in pitching.

SOUTHPAW: a left-handed pitcher.

SQUEEZE PLAY: a maneuver in which a bunt coincides with a dash for the plate by a runner on third base.

STEPS ON HIS TOES: said of a pitcher who cannot field bunts.

STRAWBERRY: an abrasion suffered in sliding.

STROLLED: drew a base on balls.

SULLIVAN: a railroad daycoach.

TAKE A LITTLE OFF: to ease off on a fast pitch.

TAKE THE BLOOD OFF IT: advice to batter who got a lucky hit.

TELEGRAPH A CURVE: some motion by a pitcher that indicates what the pitch will be.

TEXAS LEAGUER: a looping fly ball that drops safely between the infield and outfield.

TOOLS OF IGNORANCE: a catcher's equipment.

TRAFFIC COP: third-base coach.

TRUCK HORSE: a slow man.

TWO-O'CLOCK HITTER: one who hits line drives in batting practice, but pops up in games (was appropriate when game began at 3 P.M.).

UKULELE HITTER: a poor hitter.

WASTE ONE: a pitcher who deliberately throws outside the strike zone.

WHITEWASH: a shutout.

WOODEN INDIAN: batter who waits out the pitcher.

D. H.

XII. Nicknames

ANTELOPE: Emil Verban
ARCH: Paul Foytack
ARKANSAS TRAVELLER, THE:
   Travis Jackson
ARKY: Floyd Vaughn
ARRIBA: Roberto Clemente

BABE: Floyd Herman
BABE (or BAMBINO): George
   Herman Ruth
BAD BOY: Norman Sherry
BEAK, THE: Ron Hansen
BEAR: Jim Owens
BEAR, THE: Fred Hutchinson
BEAR TRACKS: Sam Mele
BIG BEAR: Mike Garcia
BIG D: Don Drysdale
BIG D: Dallas Green
BIG D: Daryl Spencer
BIG DADDY: Stan Williams
BIG KLU: Ted Kluszewski
BIG POISON: Paul Waner
BIG SIX: Christy Mathewson
BIG STU: Dick Stuart
BIG TRAIN, THE: Walter Johnson

BILLY THE KID: Billy Southworth
BINGO: Ernie Banks
BIRDIE: George Tebbetts
BLACK MIKE: Mickey Cochrane
BLAZER, THE: Don Blasingame
BLUE CHEESE: Bob Bruce
BO: Bob Belinsky
BOBO: Louis Newsom
BOBO: Larry Osborne
BOOG: John Powell
BOOG: Ralph Terry
BOOM BOOM: Willie Kirkland
BUBBA: Wycliffe Nathaniel
   Morton
BUBBA: John Phillips
BUBBLES: Gordon Coleman
BUD: Leo Daley
BULLDOG: Frank Lary

CAMERA EYE: Max Bishop
CASEY: Charles Stengel
CASPER, THE FRIENDLY GHOST:
   Jerry Adair
CAT: Harry Brecheen
CHALKY: Elio Chacon

245

COCHISE: Wally Post
COLONEL: Jim Turner
COMET: Willie Davis
COOKIE: Harry Lavagetto
COOKIE: Octavio Rojas
COUNTRY: Enos Slaughter
CRAB, THE: Johnny Evers
CROW: Frank Crosetti
CROW: William Spanswick
CUNO: Facundo Barragan

DAFFY: Paul Dean
DAZZY: Arthur Vance
DEACON: Vernon Law
DEVIL: Jim Gilliam
DIAMOND JIM: Jim Gentile
DIM-DOM-DELL: Dom
  Dallessandro
DING DONG: Gary Bell
DING DONG: Gus Bell
DIXIE: Fred R. Walker
DIZZY: Jerome Dean
DOG: Bob Skinner
DOOGIE: Bobby Del Greco
DUCKY: Dick Schofield
DUCKY: Joe Medwick
DUKE: Edwin Snider
DUMBO: Norm Larker
DUTCH: Henry Dotterer

FARMER: Bob Johnson
FAT JACK: Jack Fisher
FIDGETY: Lew Burdette
FIREBALL: Virgil Trucks
FLAKY: Jackie Brandt
FLASH: Joe Gordon
FLYING DUTCHMAN, THE: John
  Peter ("Honus") Wagner

FORDHAM FLASH, THE:
  Frank Frisch
FRENCHY: Stanley Bordagaray

GABBY: Charles Hartnett
GABBY: Bill Henry
GABBY: John Roseboro
GAR: Ed Bailey
GEORGIA PEACH, THE: Ty Cobb
GIGGI: Al Downing
GOLDEN BOY: Bill Mazeroski
GOLDEN GREEK: Alex Grammas
GOOFY: Joe Adcock
GOOFY: Vernon Gomez
GOOSE: Leon Goslin
GRANDMA: Johnny Murphy
GRAY EAGLE: Tris Speaker

HANK: Henry Aaron
HANS-A-PRANZ: Hack Wilson
HAPPY JACK: John D. Chesbro
HEAD, THE: Brooks Robinson
HONDO: Frank Howard
HONEY: John Romano
HOOKS: Warren Spahn
HOOKS: George Wiltse
HUMMER, THE: Art Fowler

IKE: Ivan Martin Delock
IRON MAN, THE: Joe McGinnity

JAKE: Alvin Powell
JAY BIRD: Jay Hook
JOLLY CHOLLY: Charlie Grimm
JOLTIN' JO-JO: George Altman
JONATHAN: Bob Friend
JUMPIN' JOE: Joe Dugan

KASKO KID, THE: Eddie Kasko
KILLER: Harmon Killebrew
KING KONG: Charles Keller

246

KITTEN: Harvey Haddix
KITTY: Jim Kaat
KOOFOO: Sandy Koufax

LARRUPIN' LOU: Lou Gehrig
LEFTY: Robert Moses Grove
LEFTY: Frank O'Doul
LIP, THE: Leo Durocher
LITTLE BULL: Orlando Cepeda
LITTLE DYNAMITE: Tony
 Gonzalez
LITTLE NAPOLEON: John
 McGraw
LITTLE NELL: Nelson Fox
LITTLE POISON: Lloyd Waner
LITTLE PROFESSOR, THE: Dom
 DiMaggio
LIZARD: Jim Bunning
LYNCH THE PINCH: Jerry Lynch

MAD RUSSIAN: Lou Novikoff
MAN, THE: Stan Musial
MAN OF A THOUSAND CURVES,
 THE: John F. Sain
MASTER MELVIN: Mel Ott
MEAL TICKET: Carl Hubbell
MEMPHIS BILL: William Terry
MEX: Hank Aguirre
MICKEY: Marv Throneberry
MIKE: Jose Miguel Fornieles
MIRACLE MAN, THE: George
 Stallings
MR. CLEAN: Dave Nicholson
MOONY: Gil Hodges
MOOSE: Eli Grba
MOOSE: Don Leppert
MOOSE: Walt Moryn
MOOSE: Paul Mosley
MOOSE: Richard Rodatz

MOOSE: Bill Skowron
MOUSY: Maury Wills

NAPOLEON: George Rucker
NONCHALONSKI: Ron Perranoski

OLD BLUE: Ray Moore
OLD FOX: Clark Griffith
OLD HOSS: Charles Radbourn
OLD PETE: Grover C. Alexander
OLD RELIABLE: Tommy Henrich
OLD ROMAN, THE: Charles
 Comiskey
OOM PAUL: Paul Derringer
ORANG OTANG: Earl Averill

PAW PAW: Charles Maxwell
PEERLESS LEADER: Frank Chance
PEE WEE: Harold Reese
PIE: Harold Traynor
PIG: Frank House
PINKY: Mike Higgins
PISTOL PETE: Pete Reiser
PLOWBOY: Tom Morgan
POINT, THE: John Podres
PREACHER: Elwood Roe
PRINCE HAL: Harold Chase
PRINCE HAL: Harold Schumacher
PROFESSOR, THE: Jim Brosnan
PROFESSOR, THE: Dick Hall
PUMPSIE: Elijah Jerry Green
PUSH-EM-UP TONY: Tony Lazzeri
PUT-PUT: Richie Ashburn

QUAIL: Bill Virdon

RABBIT, THE: Walter Maranville
RAJAH, THE: Rogers Hornsby
RAPID ROBERT: Bob Feller
ROADBLOCK: Sherman Jones
ROCKET: Ed Rakow

RUBE: John Benton
RUBE: Richard Marquard
RUBE: George Edward Waddell

SADO: Ed Sadowski
SAD SAM: Sam Jones
SAM SPADE: Elroy Face
SARGE: Charles Street
SARGE: Hoyt Wilhelm
SATCHEL: Leroy Paige
SAY HEY KID: Willie Mays
SCHNOZZ: Ernesto Lombardi
SCHOOLBOY: Lynwood T. Rowe
SCOOTER: Bob Malkmus
SCOOTER: Phil Rizzuto
SCOOTER: Bob Will
SEARS: Ed Roebuck
SHERIFF: Marshall Bridges
SLATS: Marty Marion
SLICK: Dick Howser
SLOPPY: Hollis Thurston
SLUG: Paul Richards
SMOKY: Forrest Burgess
SNAKE: Charlie Neal
SNUFFY: George Stirnweiss
SPIDER: Leonardo Cardenas
SPONGE: Roy McMillan
SPUD: Spurgeon Chandler
SQUIRREL: Roy Sievers
STONEWALL: Larry Jackson
SUDS: Norm Siebern

TATERS: Frank Lary
T-BONE: Taylor Phillips
TEX: Truman Clevenger
TITE: Luis Arroyo
TITO: John Francona
TIGER: Don Hoak
TIGER: Don Newcombe
TOOTLES: Jim O'Toole
TORO: Chuck Estrada
TURK: Omar Lown

UGLY DUCKLING: Marv Breeding
UNCLE MARV: Marvin Grissom

VINEGAR BEND: Wilmer Mizell

WAHOO SAM: Sam Crawford
WHIP, THE: Ewell Blackwell
WHISTLING WILLIE: Billy
   Williams
WHITE RAT: Whitey Herzog
WHITEY: Ed Ford
WHITEY: Carroll Lockman
WILD HORSE OF THE OSAGE, THE:
   Pepper Martin
WIMPY: Claude Osteen

YANKEE CLIPPER, THE: Joe
   DiMaggio
YATCHA: John Logan
YOGI: Lawrence Berra

ZORRO: Zoilo Versalles

D. H.

XIII. Baseball Writers

When the late Bill Slocum was covering the Yankees for the New York *American* he was in the press box in St. Petersburg one day and found himself next to a writer who was making his first trip to spring training. The questions kept coming, and Slocum kept answering them. He kept his patience, but near the end of the game it was getting more and more difficult. Finally, with the game ended, both men were busy writing their reports, when the newcomer turned to Slocum, pointed over the right-field fence, where the sun was setting, and asked, "Bill, is that the west?" Slocum looked up from his typewriter, turned to his companion and said, "Son, if it's not, you've got a helluva story."

F. G.

Hugh Fullerton, Associated Press sports department, remembers some of his dad's old favorites.

"This one," says Hugh, "was about Frank Chance coming out of the old West Side park in Chicago after losing a tough game. He was glum and mad, as usual. Mrs. Chance was waiting for him in a carriage and when he got in she said, 'Cheer up, Frank, you still have me.' 'Yeah,' said Frank, 'and I would have traded you for a base hit in the ninth inning.'

"Speaking of the West Side park just reminded me of another of Pop's stories about an Irishman who had a saloon right near there when the Cubs and White Sox played the World Series. Up to that time the Irishman had shown no interest in baseball, but when it came to the West Side vs. the South Side he got all steamed up and showed up at the ball park with half a bag on and both hands full of money wanting to make some bets.

"It went something like this: 'I'm bettin' 3 to 1 on the West Side; c'mon, you South Side so-and-sos, get your money up,' etc. It went on like that until the umpire came out to announce the batteries. He picked up a big megaphone and shouted: 'Batteries for the South Side, Walsh and Sullivan; for the West Side, Reulbach and Kling.' The Irishman was stunned into silence for a moment, then bellowed, 'Three to wan on the South Side, c'mon, you West Side,' etc.

"Incidentally, Dad told that as happening in the first game of the series but the *Red Book* shows the pitchers were Altrock and Brown and doesn't show Walsh vs. Reulbach in any game. But, as Pop used to say, 'Never let a good story be spoiled by the facts.' "

F. G.

The late, great newspaperman and magazine editor, Robert H. Davis, who, among his other achievements, was the first to give encouragement to O. Henry as a short story writer, and subsequently was a columnist on the New York *Sun* with an assignment literally to cover the world, which he did, and with distinction, said to a colleague one spring:

"I have an idea that nobody I've talked to about it likes at all. But I still think it's good. It is that ballplayers have stories that have nothing to do with baseball. What do you think?"

"I'm not sure you're right," the other said. "But let's give it a whirl. I'll tell the ballplayers you want to talk to them and set up the meetings for you ... and we'll see what happens."

Frankly, the players were more than a little scared to talk to the great man but they were assured that when they met him he would put them at their ease, being the kind of man he was, and he did. Rabbit Maranville told him of the night he'd got off the booze. Seems the night before, the Rabbit had written some letters but had gone to bed without mailing them. When he read them the next night, he discovered they were one hundred proof gibberish. On his desk in a hotel room was a quart of rye, from which he had taken only one slug. He tore up the letters ... and threw the rest of the bottle down the drain.

251

Red Lucas, a hard-nosed pitcher who would turn a dangerous hitter's cap around with a fast ball in a pinch, delighted Davis with a tale of the gratification of his ambition to grow better roses than anyone else in Columbia, Tennessee.

But perhaps Adam Comorosky, out of Swoyerville, Pennsylvania, and an outfielder with the Pirates, interested him most of all. Adam had grown up in the coal mines in a time before there were tractors to pull the carts out of the depths of the earth and he had many a tale to tell of the cussedness, the idiosyncrasies and the sly intelligence of the mine mules to thwart their drivers when they didn't feel like working.

When the series was completed and he'd given it to his colleague to read, Bob said:

"You see, you muggs don't have any imagination. All you talk to ballplayers about is baseball."

F. G.

Grantland Rice could have become a major league ballplayer if he had chosen to do so, for his hitting and his expert fielding at shortstop for Vanderbilt University caught the attention of many scouts and managers who had seen him, notably in exhibition games against Southern League clubs. Instead, he entered the newspaper field but, while working as a sports writer on the Atlanta *Journal*, played weekend games with the Atlanta Athletic Club. In one of these games, in 1905, he was deeply impressed—and for good reason—by a young left-hander pitching for a semipro team from Marietta. That night he told Ab Powell, manager of the Atlanta club in the Southern League, about him.

"His name is George Rucker and he lives in Alpharetta," Grant said. "He can make your ball club right now and some day he'll be in the big leagues."

"How did you hit against him?" Powell asked.

"He struck me out four times."

"He must be pretty good. You hit all right against Rube Waddell and some of these other pitchers in this league. Tell him to come up and I'll look at him."

Rucker had a lot of stuff but he was wild, and Powell, fighting for the Southern League pennant, had no room for him. However, he did get a job for him with the Augusta club of the Sally League, and the boy pitched a no-hit game in his first week there. Two years later he was sold to the Dodgers for delivery in 1907 and on reporting to Washington Park in Brooklyn immediately began his climb to greatness.

Rice, who, by the way, hung the Napoleon tag (subsequently shortened to Nap) on Rucker, kept pace with his protégé, reaching New York and gaining a place for himself at the very top of his profession.

F. G.

On the night of April 14, 1911, the telephone rang on the desk of Al Steimer, famous sports editor of the old New York *Herald*. Steimer could be short-tempered when he was busy and now, with another edition going to press, he was very busy.

"Yes?" he snapped into the phone.

An excited voice on the other end said:

"The Polo Grounds is on fire!"

Steimer slammed the receiver down.

"———— clowns!" he said. "Why don't they get something new? 'The Polo Grounds is on fire! A jeweler set fire to it. He wanted to get the diamond!' I shut that ———— off before he could tell me the rest of it!"

But this time it was on the level. Even as Steimer spoke,

253

there was a red glare in the Harlem sky. The wooden grandstand that John B. Day, original owner of the Giants, had taken over when the short-lived Brotherhood, formed in revolt against the National League, collapsed after the 1890 season, was burned to the ground, but the firemen saved the bleachers.

Out of the ashes rose, before the summer was out, the double-decked, steel and concrete stand conceived by John T. Brush, who then owned the club. Meanwhile, at the invitation of Frank Farrell and Bill Devery, founders of the Yankees—or Highlanders, as they then were known—the Giants played their home games at American League Park on Washington Heights.

The fire power of the Yankees made its first telling impact on the opposing clubs—and on the public—in 1921, as they battered their way to their first pennant. Babe Ruth, Bob Meusel, Wally Pipp, Home Run Baker and Elmer Miller delighted the fans in New York and depressed those in the other towns as they slugged the ball into the stands, over the fences or to the farthest corners of the fields.

On the old New York *American* at that time there was a young, gay and talented baseball writer named Arthur Robinson, whose assignment was to cover the Yankees. It was he who, awed and inspired by this thunderous crew, wrote:

"This isn't just a ball club! This is Murderers' Row!"

So the label came into being and so it has remained through the years as the original Murderers have been followed by the likes of Lou Gehrig, Tony Lazzeri, Bill Dickey, Joe DiMaggio, Charley Keller, Tommy Henrich, Johnny Mize, Yogi Berra, Mickey Mantle, and Roger Maris.

In the time of the Ruth-Meusel-Gehrig-Lazzeri combine there was a pitcher by the name of Grady Adkins with the

White Sox. This—it would be along about 1927—was his first year in the league and he hadn't pitched against the Yankees and now they were moving into Chicago and he was told that he would face them in the opening game of the series. Moe Berg was a catcher with the Sox then and Adkins said to him before the game:

"Tell me, Moe. Are the Yankees really so tough?"

"Tough?" Moe said. "Sure they are, but only for sucker pitchers. Now, a pitcher of your class has nothing to fear from them. Disregard anything you may have heard about them. Just go in there and pitch as you have against the other clubs and they'll do you no harm."

Young Adkins did. That is, he pitched against the Yankees as he had against the other clubs. Before he'd got anybody out, the Yankees had three runs and there were two of them on the bases, leering at him. Beckoned out of the box by the manager, Ray Schalk, he walked in fury to the dugout on his way to the clubhouse and, pausing on the steps of the dugout, he glared at Berg and said:

"You lied to me! I'll never speak to you again as long as I live!"

And there was, in that time, Rube Lutzke, third baseman of the Cleveland club. This day, in Cleveland, Joe Ben Shaute, one of the top pitchers in either league, started against the Yankees. Earle Combs, leading off, drilled a low liner that caromed off Rube's shins. Mark Koenig bounced one off his left knee. The Babe, slicing one down the third-base line, narrowly missed tearing his head off. Meusel hit him squarely in the belly with a blazer. As he lay on his back, gasping for breath, Shaute ran over to him and asked, anxiously:

"Are you hurt, Rube?"

255

And the Rube snarled:

"Hurt? You ————! A guy would be safer in a world war!"

F. G.

Long John Reilly was the only big league player in history to be shipwrecked on his way to his team. He was believed lost when the steamship *Narragansett* burned after colliding with the *Stonington* on Long Island Sound. Reilly, a member of the Cincinnati Reds (this was on June 12, 1880), was in the water one hour, then was picked up and taken to New York. Left with only an undershirt, socks and pants, he sat on the wharf from 11 A.M. to 4 P.M. before clothing was given him.

LEE ALLEN

Early glimpse of the Pittsburgh Pirates. When this team joined the American Association, then a major league, in 1882, the players, officially known as the Alleghenies, called themselves the "Slaughterhouse Nine."

"Let's slide out to the slaughterhouse," a player would say before a game, or, "It's just twenty minutes till killing time."

LEE ALLEN

When I was five years old my mother was going to a hospital and she told me that when she came back she would have another brother or sister for me and that, meanwhile, friends of hers had asked if I might stay with them while she was away. I didn't want to go at first because I didn't want to leave my father and my grandmother and my brother and sister but I was very glad that I did.

The friends were Dave Bancroft of the New York Giants and his wife, Edna, a very beautiful woman, and I called them Uncle Dave and Aunt Edna. Living with them was living in a child's paradise. They had an apartment in the Croydon, a residential hotel near Central Park, and every evening when Uncle Dave came home (there was no night baseball then) he would have a present for me. We went out to dinner nearly every night, even though we had a kitchen in the apartment. The kitchen had swinging doors, like an old-fashioned saloon (my father told me) and Uncle Dave and I played a little game every evening. I would lock the doors and he would pretend he couldn't get out and then I would crawl under the doors and tell him to follow me to safety. When I grew old enough to realize what a famous ballplayer he was, I wondered what the fans would have thought if they could have seen him crawling on the floor with a five-year-old girl!

There was a great day when Aunt Edna took me to the Polo Grounds. I do not remember whom the Giants were playing but there was a big crowd there and Uncle Dave, who was the shortstop and captain of the team, came over to the field box where we were seated to say hello to us. Aunt Edna bought me a hot dog and some chewing gum. There were two games that day and between games, she took me up to the press box to see my father, who was a baseball writer. She stood me on a chair and I was wearing a yellow dress and a straw hat she had bought me and all the baseball writers came to say hello to me and ask me how I was and I remember I kept saying: "Fine! Fine!"

I was glad to see my father but I also was glad when the second game started so that I could go back and watch Uncle Dave play. Do you wonder that I grew up to be a Giant fan and to think that the Polo Grounds was the greatest ball park in the land?

MARY GRAHAM

257

No baseball writer ever was closer to John McGraw than Sam Crane, who covered the New York Giants for the old *Evening Journal* from the late nineties to the day of his death in the summer of 1925 at the age of seventy-one. He had picked up what he thought was no more than a heavy cold in Cincinnati, last stop on a Western trip, and died a few days after the club returned to New York.

Maybe the strong bond between him and McGraw was forged in the circumstance that he, too, had been a ballplayer in the National League, although not a contemporary of McGraw's in that field, for he was nineteen years older and an established baseball writer at the Polo Grounds when McGraw arrived as manager in 1902. They had many things in common, such as baseball, a quick temper, a liking for bridge and good whiskey. So they worked together, played cards together, drank together, and on occasion, abused each other roundly.

Their quarrels, which always occurred after sundown, invariably were launched by McGraw, sometimes in earnest, sometimes just for fun. Sam, being an honest reporter, would belt his friend in print when he thought his friend had made a tactical error that had cost the Giants a ball game and McGraw would pick him up on that and savage him. Or it might be, in the beginning, that John simply was needling Sam—and no one could thrust a needle deeper. However it started, in earnest or in jest, the result always was the same although, of course, by morning the bitter words that had passed between them had been forgotten. Remembered here is a night in McGraw's drawing room on a train out of St. Louis when Sam, who really had been baited, got up in anger and started for the door.

"Sit down," McGraw said, "and have a drink."

258

HOT STOVE LEAGUE

"————!" Sam shouted. "I'll never take another drink with you as long as I live!"

By this time he was at the door and, wheeling, he fired an afterthought:

"Till tomorrow night!"

F. G.

Once upon a time—and it was a time he likes to remember—Ford Frick, Commissioner of Baseball, was a baseball writer covering the Yankees. This was in the twenties and early thirties when the Yankees, on their visits to Chicago, made their headquarters at the Del Prado Hotel on the South Side lake front. Hard by was the Chicago Beach Hotel, where Kenesaw Mountain Landis, first of the Commissioners, lived and there would be evenings (there was no night baseball then) that Ford would suggest to a couple of other writers:

"Let's walk over and see the Judge."

The Judge and Mrs. Landis always would receive them graciously and they'd always have a pleasant evening, listening to the Judge's stories of his boyhood in Indiana, which were especially interesting to Ford, a Hoosier, too. And of some of his amusing experiences with the club owners who, although he was in their pay, lived in constant fear of him while he, for his part, despised them.

Who could have guessed that one day Ford would succeed to the high office then filled by the aging gentleman for whom he had such an abiding affection? Surely not Ford. He didn't even want it when, years later, it was thrust upon him. Yet, looking back, he must recall many things the Judge told him out of his own experiences that helped to guide him in the performance of his duties.

F. G.

During the baseball meetings in New York in February of 1934, Roscoe McGowen of the *New York Times* asked a question of Bill Terry and received an answer that had a direct bearing on the outcome of the National League race that year. Terry, then the manager of the world champion Giants, was holding an impromptu press conference in the lobby of the Hotel Roosevelt and, as he discussed his views of his own club and its chief rivals, Roscoe wanted to know:

"How about Brooklyn, Bill?"

The Dodgers had finished sixth in 1933 and Terry grinned and asked:

"Brooklyn? Is Brooklyn still in the league?"

Everybody laughed—and everybody printed the crack. It created amusement everywhere but in Brooklyn, where it was violently resented. Casey Stengel, who unexpectedly had succeeded Max Carey as manager of the Dodgers before the opening of the season, shrewdly fashioned it into a weapon which he turned against the Giants by rousing his generally inept players to a degree where they reached a peak of ferocity every time they tangled with their interborough rivals. And, as they badgered and sometimes wounded the Giants, the Brooklyn fans noisily reviled Terry.

Ironically, the season ended on this note: The Cardinals and the Giants had but two games each to play, the Cardinals with the Reds in St. Louis and the Giants with the Dodgers at the Polo Grounds on a Saturday and Sunday. If the Cardinals won and the Giants lost on Saturday, they could get no worse than a tie even if they lost on Sunday and the Giants won. Bedlam was the word for the Polo Grounds that Saturday, for if the Dodger fans present didn't outnumber the Giant fans in a crowd of 50,000, they at least made more noise and the Dodgers, inspired by their enthusiasm, beat the Giants while, in St. Louis, the Cardinals beat the Reds. Now, on Sunday, the turbulent scene was repeated—and so was the outcome. The Dodgers won— and so did the Cardinals, and Terry's flippant reply to Mc- Gowen had come back to haunt him as the Gas House Gang moved toward the World Series with the Tigers.

F. G.

Most baseball writers are like most people and there have been eccentrics among them, too. One was the late Bill Phelon of the Cincinnati *Times-Star,* who kept a small alligator in a bathtub in his home, carried a squirrel in his jacket pocket around the National League circuit, and once showed up in the press box at the Polo Grounds bearing a small cardboard box with air holes punched in the cover.

"What's in the box?" Granny Rice asked.

"A fer-de-lance," Bill said happily. "A friend of mine brought him to me."

Webster defines a fer-de-lance as "a poisonous snake in- habiting certain of the West Indies and the South American countries."

F. G.

The late William B. Hanna was one of the best of all base- ball writers in his time on the old *Herald,* the old *Sun,* and the old *Tribune* in New York. Old, all of them? Yes, and so was Bill Hanna when he died. How old was he? No one knew, for he wasn't telling, but there was a morning on a train bearing the New York Giants into St. Louis and all the berths had been made up and Bill was sitting with another writer and, as the train rolled through the freight yards, he said:

"I painted boxcars in these yards so long ago that it seems like another existence."

263

Now, for a moment, he was lost in reverie and then he said:

"Once I was a waiter in a hashhouse in Butte, Montana, where a nickel was big tip."

Bill Hanna painting boxcars in a St. Louis freight yard? Bill Hanna taking nickel tips off tables in a hashhouse in Butte? It seemed incredible to one who had known him for ten years or more and had heard from those who had known him much longer that his was of one of the first families of Kansas City and that in one period of his newspaper career he had taken a two-year leave of absence to enroll in a course in archaeology at Harvard and go with an expedition to Egypt to dig in the tombs of the Pharaohs.

He was a little man, only this tall and this wide, and wherever he bought his clothes, his tailor must have been proud of him, for he wore them well. He was crotchety and, although he was one of the greatest of baseball writers, he had no regard for the players.

"Clods!" he once said. "Clods, all of them!"

His skills as a writer took him beyond baseball. Football was within his province. So was billiards. Jack Doyle once said of him:

"He is the only one I've ever known who could write a column and a half account of a billiard match and hold the reader's interest to the last line."

And Chick Meehan, then the football coach at New York University and Bill's constant friend and bedside watcher to the day he breathed his last, said:

"You know, Bill died without ever realizing what a great sports writer he was."

The old ones in the sports writing business sometimes speak of him, even now, yet the pity of it is that they remember only one line he spoke. Not one that he wrote, mind you.

It was in the spring of 1924 and the New York Giants were training in Sarasota, Florida. They had scheduled an exhibition game with the Reds in Orlando and Bill asked another writer:

"Are you going to the game?"

"Yes," the other said.

"Why?" Bill asked.

"Well, for two reasons," the other said. "It's my job to cover the game—and I've never been to Orlando and I'd like to see it."

"You won't like it," Bill said.

"I won't? Why?"

"Too many trees," Bill said.

That is the line they remember and that has been handed down by them to the young ones.

F. G.

John Kieran, naturalist, author and wit, was a baseball writer and, later, general sports columnist for the *New York Times* on his way to fame in a broader range of operations. As such, he justly had the respect not only of his colleagues but of the managers and players in both major leagues. Among his many friends and admirers was Stanley Harris who, in 1929, was managing the Washington Senators. The Yankees had won the pennant in the three previous seasons —and two World Series, too, so that they dominated not only the American League but the National League as well—but now, hard pressed by the Philadelphia Athletics in early September, they were fading fast.

John dropped in on Harris in the Senators' dugout at the Yankee Stadium one day and asked him:

"Who do you think will win the pennant?"

"The A's," Stanley said, "and I hate to think of it."

"Why?"

"Because," Stanley said, "they're a lot of swellheaded stiffs now and if they win they'll be impossible."

The Senators left that night for Philadelphia where, on the following day, they opened a series in a double-header. Subsequently, Stanley said:

"The moment I showed up on the field, the crowd booed me. I was puzzled, but flattered, by their attention, for they hadn't even noticed me for four years, since we'd won our last pennant. Every time, during the first game, I so much as stuck my head out of the dugout, they gave it to me—but good, and I wondered what it was all about until, between games, a Philadelphia writer showed me a clipping of John's interview with me, which had been picked up by all the local papers.

"He asked me if I had been correctly quoted and I said:

" 'Of course. You know John Kieran and you know he doesn't misquote anybody.'

"To tell the truth, I was somewhat startled to see my words in print because I had assumed John and I were just carrying on a conversation and didn't know he was going to quote me."

"Well," somebody said, "you sure stood up for him, as, being the man you are, you would."

"Stand up, hell!" Stanley said. "John is my friend and I had said exactly what he wrote. What would you expect me to do?"

"Exactly what you did, and when I see John I'll tell him about it."

"Tell him nothing," Stanley said, "except that I enjoyed his story and thought it was one of the best he ever wrote."

F. G.

266

There was a chilling background to the return to baseball writing of Big Ed Burns of the Chicago *Tribune*. As a reporter on the city staff, his beat was the Federal Courthouse which meant, in the early twenties, covering arrests, examinations, or trials of bootleggers apprehended by the Feds, and, consequently, he got to know many of the bigshot mobsters.

One afternoon, as he was walking on Wabash Avenue in the Loop, a car pulled up at the curb and one of two men in it called out:

"Hi, Ed! Where are you going? Can we give you a lift?"

It was Schemer Drucchi, a wily and vicious thug who was credited—if that's the word for it—with having devised "the ride" as a method of luring an unsuspecting rival, or even a fellow gang member, into a one-way trip to a spot where his body would be found, sooner or later.

Ed had no fear of Drucchi and, in other circumstances, might have accepted the invitation to a lift but his destination was just around the corner and he declined with thanks. The Schemer, however, was in a talkative mood and several minutes passed before Ed could break away from him.

The following day he was hailed in a corridor of the courthouse by a member of a mob that was at war with Drucchi's.

"Take a tip from me," the mobster said. "Stay away from the Schemer."

Eddie must have appeared puzzled by the warning.

"Remember when he stopped you on Wabash Avenue yesterday?"

"Oh, yes, of course."

"Some of our boys were trailing him in a car. He must have spotted them and seen you at the same time. That's why he stopped you. He knew our boys wouldn't hit him

267

then because one of them might have hit you. He figured right and they backed off. But next time you might not be so lucky."

When Ed reached his office late in the afternoon he told the city editor what had happened.

"It seems," he said, "I am getting too well known for my own good. I used to write baseball in my home down in Indiana and I think I'd like to go back to it."

And so a transfer to the sports staff was arranged for him and he became one of the drollest of all baseball writers and a tremendous favorite with the *Tribune*'s readers, and the ballplayers too.

F. G.

Well, there it is, up to now, an informal view of the wits and the wise men who have had so large a part in shaping a period of the history of a sport that, you might say, came out of nowhere—or everywhere that man first found joy in hitting a ball with a stick.

They have known laughter and tears and victory and defeat, have solved some of their problems and hopelessly muddled others. Walking with them through the years have been artists and writers who have tried earnestly to pin them down, with brush or pen and ink or in type, as characters very like you and me, except that they could pitch better, hit better and field better.

They came from the farms, the villages, the towns or the sandlots or public parks of the big cities. Some of them, in life or death, wound up in Cooperstown, baseball's version of Valhalla, but even the least of them, each in his own fashion, has earned remembrance.

F. G.